The Dobson 14-Day Method of Dog Training

The Dobson
14-Day
Method of
Dog Training

Joseph A. Dobson

Winchester Press
Tulsa, Oklahoma

Library of Congress Cataloging in Publication Data

Dobson, Joseph A
    The Dobson 14-day method of dog training.

    Includes index.
    1. Dogs—Training. I. Title.
II. Title: 14-day method of dog training.
SF431.D62   636.7′0887   80-26724
ISBN 0-87691-334-6

Printed in the United States of America

Winchester Press
1421 South Sheridan
P.O. Box 1260
Tulsa, Oklahoma 74101

Book design: Susan Trail

1 2 3 4 5   85 84 83 82 81

To my loving father

Walter R. Dobson, Sr.

who was my dearest friend, companion, and teacher

and to my wonderful wife

Joan

for the endless hours she devoted to helping
make this book possible

My thanks to photographer

Shawn M. Pickett

for his time and effort in taking the training illustration
photographs for this book.

Introduction

For years I have been beseiged by dog owners, professional trainers, and dog club members to write a book on my method of speed-training dogs. I have never planned to teach my method, which took me many years to develop, and I cherished it as much as the chef prizes his secret recipes. However, since so many people have asked for information about my fast, precision training method, I finally decided it would be a waste of knowledge not to make it available to the many others who wish to learn it.

I began learning animal training over 40 years ago. My father was a proficient trainer in his own right and taught me a great deal. We did many different types of training with dogs, such as scent work, retrieving, guard, trick work, hunting, herding, and man trailing. In those days, dogs were trained in the open fields. They often had to work at long distances from their handler. Consequently, they had to be well trained and able to take their commands by voice, horn, whistle, or hand signal.

One of the things that interested me most was the differences in the personality and mental attitude of each animal. My experiences from working with different dogs, as well as various wild and domestic animals, made it possible for me to understand animals and train them more quickly and efficiently.

Over the years of studying each dog closely, using psychology, and experimenting with various ways of teaching a particular exercise, I was able to train a dog in less and less time. Today I can train any of my dogs to work off leash on both hand and voice commands on all basic work and on much of the advanced obedience work in a matter of a few days.

The trainability of each animal varies according to its intelligence and memory retention and how well it applies its powers of observation and concentration. Throughout this book, I talk about how a dog "thinks." Only man is supposed to have the ability to reason, but scientific experiments have provided evidence that some of the higher animals can solve simple problems by a mental process that amounts to elementary reasoning—not trial and error, not instinct or reflex, not training, but reasoning. Dogs react in different ways to different situations, and some dogs are smarter than others. The important thing to remember is that a dog has a brain and emotions, and his response to a command definitely involves a mental process. If you want to train a dog quickly and successfully, you'll have to grant that he thinks and then make your approach conform to *how* he thinks.

Conventional obedience training is divided into three courses: novice (basic), open, and utility (dog show competition). Novice training normally requires 10 to 12 weeks of daily training. The intermediate and advanced courses require 4 months each. My obedience training consists of all novice training, part of open and utility, as well as other exercises not taught in usual obedience work. The dog also learns hand signals and should be able to perform all exercises off leash (and at distances) in only 14 days. Each day the dog learns a new exercise and receives practice on the earlier lessons.

For successful training in 14 days, the owner must be prepared to devote 1½ to 2 hours per day to the dog. During the first few days of training, lessons can be as short as 1 hour. As the dog learns more exercises, a longer period is necessary to give him sufficient practice on all commands.

Many dog owners find it hard to believe that obedience training can really be accomplished so quickly. As proof that this method works, I'd like to quote from a letter of appreciation written in 1981 by one of my customers, Nabil Koudsi, M.D. Dr. Koudsi, a California heart surgeon who had acquired a German shepherd pup, made the following comments: "When I took my 4-month-old pup to Joseph Dobson, I was skeptical that the animal could be trained for obedience in 14 days. When the 2-week period was up, I was amazed and totally pleased with the results."

Just as some dogs are smarter than others, some owners (or trainers) are smarter than others. Someone who has had much experience will have an advantage, although anyone can train a dog in 14 days using this method. The point is that the better the trainer, the more thoroughly the dog will be trained at the end of the 14 days.

This training method makes it possible to produce a well-trained dog in an unheard-of short time, 2 weeks, as compared with the normal months of work for the same amount of training. In addition to being much faster with infinitely superior results, it is much easier for both dog and trainer and can improve the performance of any dog. Dogs as young as 4 months of age and older dogs of any age can be trained with this method. For those owners who do not go on to additional training, this course still provides the know-how to produce a well-trained, obedient dog with a greatly improved personality.

Contents

Introduction, vii

Basics of Training, 1

Training Tips, 11

Reactions of Dogs to Training, 15

The 14-Day Dog Training Method, 23

Lesson 1

Heeling with Automatic Sit Exercise, 32

Lesson 2

Sit/Stay Exercise, 37

Lesson 3

Down Exercise, Away from Dog, 43

Lesson 4

Down and Sit Exercise, Away from Dog and at Heel Position, 48

Lesson 5

Come (Recall) and Finish Exercise, 53

Lesson 6

Stay While Heeling Exercise (Motion Exercise), 61

Lesson 7

Beginning Distance Training, 65

Lesson 8

Beginning Off-Leash Work, 69

Lesson 9

Stand Exercise, 75

Lesson 10

Teaching the Dog to Come When Not On Command and Starting Distraction Work, 80

Lesson 11

Down (Drop) on Recall (Motion Exercise), 88

Lesson 12

Sit on Recall (Motion Exercise), 92

Lesson 13

Stay on Recall (Motion Exercise), 95

Lesson 14

Off-Leash Distraction Work, 99

Training Problems, 103

Appendix

Photo Review of Training Exercises, 123

Index, 146

Basics of Training

Training is any method by which an animal learns something. Everyone learns from the day he is born, either from watching others and imitating them or from listening to parents or friends. A puppy begins learning from the day he is brought into the home. He may not learn what you want him to, but he is constantly learning something. For an animal to learn specific behaviors, he must be taught. He can learn anything, provided he is properly taught in a manner he can understand.

Many times, I have heard a dog owner say that his dog is too "dumb" to learn anything. Usually, the real cause of the problem is the owner who does not know how to teach the dog. Just as the dog needs to be taught what you want him to know, a person needs to be taught to train a dog. People are not born with the knowledge to train a dog, they must learn from another person, a book, or trial-and-error—which may not be successful. Much of the dog training in past years was based on methods used for training horses and was not entirely suited to dogs. Dog psychology was seldom used or even understood. Some methods were merely efforts by the trainer to get the dog to "catch on" by encouraging numerous "guessing" attempts by the dog.

Most trainers have learned only one way to teach a dog a particular exercise. This method is not always successful, since no two dogs are alike. Therefore, if a lesson is presented to a dog in a manner he cannot grasp, he may not be able to learn it at all or he may require considerably more time and effort. Frequently, dog owners working in a group class will take their dogs through the same course two or three times before the dogs can finally do the exercises very well.

Owners often complain about their "problem" dogs, but they do not realize the problem is their own creation. The dog knows only what he learns on his own or what he is taught. He is not born with bad habits; they are created. If a person expects his dog to possess desirable traits, he must teach the dog what he wants him to know. If the owner doesn't know how to teach, he must either learn or have someone else teach the dog. For the additional pleasure he gives throughout his life, a well-trained dog is worth the effort or expense.

Most of the methods currently used in dog training are time-consuming, tiring, and boring. Few dogs are trained for various duties because present methods are too slow to produce results. If a dog were selected for several types of training, he would be too old to be of any practical use by the time he was trained. With the short-cut methods I have developed, a young dog can be trained for many types of work.

Many people ask how old a dog should be to be trained. It is rather pointless to begin training a very old dog. They are set in their ways and changes are more difficult for them to make. Most dogs can begin training at about 4 months of age. Their mind is normally quite well-developed, and their attention span is reasonably good. Older dogs can, of course, be trained at any time. However, the older the dog, the more bad habits it has acquired.

Dog Psychology

The subject of dog psychology could fill a book. A basic understanding of it is necessary for anyone who wishes to train a dog properly and quickly.

Understanding the dog plays an important part in the actual training. Proper training brings the dog closer to you, creating a new and wonderful relationship, a common bond that didn't exist before. Poor training can have the reverse effect and do permanent damage to the dog's personality and temperament.

Surprisingly, many dog trainers have little or no knowledge of dog psychology. They are concerned only with finishing the training. If the dog is not mentally able to cope with their methods, they don't care. The dog is then simply labeled *dumb* or *untrainable*. A good trainer is an artist. He takes pride in his finished product, which he molds with care, adapting and adjusting his methods to the dog's personality and temperament to produce a well-trained dog with a sounder, more fully rounded personality.

Dogs are like people in many ways. They come in many different types, sizes, and shapes and also with many different personalities, intelligence levels, and dispositions. Because of these differences, each dog is an individual—even pups from the same litter. Dogs also have various emotions: love, hate, anger, fear, surprise. They think about various things that interest or concern them, and they dream when they sleep. Another similarity to man is that dogs have facial expressions, and their eyes display worry, fear, happiness, surprise, and anger. By studying your dog and watching his eyes, facial expressions, and actions, you can learn many things. Even though he cannot talk, he often tries to show you what he is thinking.

Dogs use a sign language among themselves and often attempt to use it with their masters. An observant dog owner or trainer can learn to understand this language. Many of the misunderstandings about dogs and the difficulties encountered in training are a result of the communication gap between dog and owner, and most people do not know how to bridge it. A mute, without special training, would also have difficulty communicating, but this does not mean that he is stupid or can't think.

Locking eyes (staring) is a threat and challenge in dog sign language. When two dogs do this, a fight is certain to follow. If a person stares directly at the eyes of a dog, particularly a strange dog, the dog is likely to bite the person. Often, a dog will not accept this challenge from someone he knows and likes and will indicate this by turning his head. Frequently, a person is bitten for no apparent reason, probably because he stared at the eyes of the dog without realizing it and without knowing the effect it had.

Another interesting behavioral aspect of the dog is submission. Frequently when approached by another dog, a dog will lie down, which means that he is surrendering. A dog does this for many reasons. A pup will lie down to let the other dog know he merely wishes to play and is not offering a challenge. An older dog will sometimes lie down when he is away from his home grounds and is approached by another dog to show that he does not wish to dispute the other's territorial boundary nor fight to determine who is in authority. Another reason for this behavior is that the dog feels outnumbered or outclassed.

When a dog cowers and/or lies down for his owner, such as when he is being yelled at or when the owner is showing intent to strike, it means the same: the dog is giving up and wishes to be spared any punishment. Some dogs will lie down when they are being trained because the trainer is being too rough and not praising and petting enough to give the dog confidence and trust. Other dogs, if pressed too far with continued punishment after they have attempted to surrender, may turn vicious, since begging for mercy did no good.

The dog world has its own form of hierarchy and each member must conform to the unwritten rules and regulations or trouble begins. These laws are normally followed by nearly all dogs. If a bitch (female dog) has a newborn litter, a male will usually give her wide berth. If he comes too close to her quarters and she attacks him, the male will run because he knows he is off-limits. Even though he may be physically capable of overpowering her, he knows that under these circumstances, the bitch will not give an inch and will fight to her last breath if necessary.

When two or more dogs are kept together, one dog, usually the older, is always the boss. Even though a younger dog may be bigger, stronger, bolder, and more aggressive, he will usually give way to the older dog's honorable position of authority but may assume second in command. If the younger or newer dog challenges the authority of the boss, he will be reprimanded immediately.

A dog's state of mind has great impact on his training. A person purchasing a new dog that is old enough to train should not attempt to begin immediately. The dog needs to adjust to a new home environment and new people. This in itself is a mental strain on the dog, without immediately beginning formal training and thereby increasing the stress. Likewise, never attempt to work a dog that is sick or has anything physically wrong with it that could cause discomfort or pain. A dog cannot concentrate on his lessons when he does not feel his best.

The dog has tremendous powers of concentration, the depth of which can be so intense that it is possible for him to see, hear, and feel nothing else—including pain—when his mind is completely locked on something that deeply interests him. For a trainer to obtain the greatest success, he must be able to hold the dog's interest.

The dog must not be upset while he is being trained. If he is frightened, nervous, or worried, his trainability is greatly reduced because his mind is not open and his concentration is impaired. Intense or continued mental stress reduces his ability to learn and can damage his mind, personality, and disposition. Just as in people, the mental and emotional strength of each dog varies. Consequently, nervous or timid dogs must be handled carefully because they have a very low breaking point, thereby making them poor training subjects. It is also possible for a sound dog to become unsound by improper handling or training.

Any person training a dog must never lose his temper when working with the dog. The dog immediately knows when the person is upset, which, in turn, upsets the animal. If the trainer is losing his self-control, the lesson should be ended until the trainer can regain his composure, be it an hour or a day. An angry person who attempts to work with a dog may ruin the good work he has already done. Patience is said to be a virtue, but it is a *necessity* for the dog trainer.

If a dog becomes tired, bored, or upset during a lesson (usually indicated by the dog repeatedly lying down, getting restless, or looking away), stop the lesson. Tension will often build up in the dog from the strain of trying to absorb what he is being taught. When this occurs, a couple of 10-minute rest breaks can give him time to relax and collect himself. Then he will usually be more cooperative and enthusiastic about the lesson. After the lesson, play with the dog. During rest and play periods, talk to your dog, pet him, and feed him a few snacks. This improves his frame of mind and gives him a mental uplift.

The dog recalls the events of the day, his activities, and those things that happened to him that made a deep impression. For this reason, I like to have a dog undisturbed or at least not upset between his daily lessons so his thoughts will be on his training. Some dogs are more impressionable than others and can become upset and emotionally disturbed just from harsh words. Abuse, fear, pain, and scoldings make a deep impression on a dog, causing emotional upset and stress that affect his training, concentration, ability to learn, personality, and behavior.

Bad emotional experiences can only be erased by time and pleasant experiences. A dog that had been doing well on his commands can suddenly develop a mental block and be unable to do commands he previously knew. A mental block occurs when a dog is handled roughly and he doesn't understand why. This block can be the result of any type of physical pain or scolding or the trainer correcting too hard or too often. If the dog is being handled correctly in training and a mental block develops, it is usually because of something that happened to the dog during his leisure hours. Do not hamper your training by permitting the dog to be mishandled by anyone.

If a dog has developed a mental block since its previous lesson, it is readily apparent as soon as the training lesson begins. When a command is given, the dog won't know what to do. For example, a dog that has been doing commands well suddenly doesn't know whether to sit at your left side or your right; he may look in another direction when you give him a command; he may lie down when you command him to heel; or he may come to you, crouching, when you command him to stay. When this happens, do *not* start correcting the dog harshly. Instead, try to calm him down. Sit and talk to him for awhile. Then start working him again, gently. If he still can't do his commands, you may have to end the lesson for that day. Play with him for awhile and try to calm him. Usually, the next day the dog will work as well as he did previously.

If a trainer gets rough with an upset dog, there can be several repercussions. The dog may attempt to bite the trainer, or he may attempt to run away. The dog will definitely take a big setback in his training and may develop a permanent mental block about one or more of his commands, resulting in confusion. The dog may also fear his trainer and/or hate his exercises.

A dog does not really understand commands until he has completed his training. To make fast progress in his training, avoid confusing him about his commands. While a dog is being trained, his commands *should not* be used for anything but his lessons. If he does something wrong, smack him on the nose with a newspaper or magazine and tell him "No!" but do not use any of the words in his commands to reprimand him, such as yelling at him to lie down or sit down. His training commands are to be used in training *only*.

The trainability of different dogs varies considerably. The very nervous, timid dog is undoubtedly the poorest training subject. I have found that bold, aggressive dogs make the best training prospects. They are sometimes harder to work with in the beginning because of their dominant personality, but once the trainer establishes his authority, they are considerably more rewarding. They are the most intelligent of all dogs, quicker to learn and with considerably greater memory retention. They are also more alert and observant, which enhances their trainability.

The intelligence of a dog has a great deal to do with its trainability. All dogs in the middle categories are trainable, in varying degrees. The easy-going, placid dog is usually lazy and somewhat indifferent to his surroundings, making him less energetic and more difficult to train because he is inclined to be inattentive. The spirited, active, sometimes mischievous dog makes a good training subject. These dogs are often a problem as an untrained companion because they abound with energy and always seem to be into something. They are usually fast workers and enjoy having something to do. The particularly sharp-eyed, observant dog will study his trainer extremely carefully and learn to watch closely for any habits, movements, or actions that might be clues to the trainer's next move. It is often difficult to keep up with this type of dog, let alone outsmart or outguess him.

Many dogs can analyze man. They can recognize variations in human moods and emotions and can readily interpret them. They learn and recognize many things about the people they know, including the sound of their footsteps, the sound of their car's motor, their reaction to certain situations, their habits, and even the time they arrive home from work. The dog actually spends more time and effort studying his human contacts than the human does studying the dog.

Training Equipment

The equipment you will need for obedience training is minimal; however, I highly recommend that you do not scrimp on these items. Buy good-quality merchandise that will last and not break the second or third time you use it.

First of all, you will need a six-foot leather leash that is of a good grade and thickness of leather with a sturdy swivel bolt snap. The snap should be sturdy, preferably solid brass, which does not break. Strap leather is much better than latigo, which is very stretchy and is soon only half the width it was when new. If you are unable to find a good cowhide leash and must use latigo, buy a width wider than suggested for the size of your dog (small, toys, ½ inch; medium, ⅝ inch; large, ¾ inch; giant, 1 inch). I personally prefer to use a size larger than the minimum suggested, because the leash will have a larger snap, which is useful in several corrections.

You will also need a short leather leash that is only 8 to 12 inches long. If you cannot find one, make one out of an old leash by adding a swivel bolt snap just below the hand loop on the leash. If you are unable to fasten the snap, any shoe repairman can sew it on for you.

The last item needed is the metal choke collar—a small chain with a ring on each end. Several types and sizes are sold by pet suppliers, but the one I insist on is a single-strand, American-made, welded steel choker. These normally come in three link sizes: fine, medium, and large. The large link has oval, semitwisted links about ⅞ inch long and ½ inch wide. If you think this is too heavy for toy breeds, you may prefer to use the medium-sized link, which is ½ inch long and ⅜ inch wide. However, the smaller the link, the more painful it can be on corrections. *Never* use a fine-link choke collar on any dog. The medium-link choke collar is sometimes used on dogs that have built up a tough neck, particularly larger dogs and pain-insensitive dogs, or on dogs trained by a small or weak person who cannot give a good correction. Use only the amount of force necessary to accomplish the purpose; neither overdo nor underdo it, as will be explained more fully in the chapters on training. The large-link choke collar applies pressure; the smaller links cut or peel the skin, particularly on a soft neck.

Also consider the proper length of the choke collar. Normally, you should purchase a length that will slip over the dog's head easily but not be so loose that it can fall off when he lowers his head. For training, however, use a choke collar that is approximately 2 to 4 inches longer than normal, which allows for a good amount of slack. For example, for a young German Shepherd who normally wears a 22-inch choke collar, switch to a 24- or 26-inch choke collar for lessons. This choke collar is not left on the dog after the lesson; it is strictly for training.

To put the choke collar on the dog, attach the snap of the leash to one ring of the choke collar. Hold the ring with the leash snap attached in the air, letting the loose ring hang. Grasp this loose ring with the fingers of your other hand as you drop the chain through the center of this loose ring. When the entire chain has passed through this ring, right up to the opposite ring where the leash is attached, a noose is formed. Holding the upper portion of this noose, turn it so the ring holding the leash snap is on your left hand, still maintaining the noose with the choke collar. Be sure the end of the chain nearest the ring with the leash attached is at the top. If held correctly, the circle of chain will be hanging from your hand; the free ring will be next to the ring that has the leash snap attached. Face the dog and slip the noose over his head. Check to see that the leash end of the choke collar is lying across the back of the dog's neck. If the choke collar is put on correctly, it will tighten around the dog's neck when you lift up the leash; when you slacken the leash, the choke collar should loosen. When a sharp jerk is applied with the leash, the choke collar will "slap" the muscles on the sides of the dog's neck. If the choke collar is put on incorrectly, the leash will pinch the throat when pulled and will not be slack when loosened.

A long leash, a short leash, and a choke collar are the only equipment you will need. Several other pieces of equipment are used by many trainers, but I do not find them necessary. The lounge-line is not practical in my training method since the dog is quickly switched to off-leash work. The throw chain, which is frequently used to strike the dog, will panic him. While some dogs can be taught to come with its use, other dogs have the opposite reaction; once hurt by it, they attempt to run away the next time. Continued use of the throw chain on a dog that is not psychologically capable of enduring this type of correction can harm his personality as well as prolong training or make it impossible to teach the Come exercise at all.

Common Training Mistakes

Trainer mistakes defeat your purpose, confuse the dog, and considerably slow down the training process because it is difficult for the dog to understand what is expected of him. Commands must be kept simple so the dog can learn them. Most commands consist of only one word, together with the dog's name. The name of the dog always precedes the command word, such as "Rex, sit!" Verbal commands and hand signals must always be used *exactly the same*. People working with a dog will often change the command or add to it without even realizing it, such as "Rex, get over there and sit!" or "Rex, come here and lie down" or "Rex, I said down!" You cannot expect the dog to learn a command if you vary or change it in any way.

The trainer must pay attention to what he is doing with his hands when working the dog. The dog must learn certain hand movements; therefore, do not confuse him with unnecessary gestures.

Do not try to force an idea on a dog. Not every dog can learn a particular exercise in the same length of time or in the same manner. A dog may learn a certain exercise with little effort but may have trouble learning another exercise. Some trainers recommend repeated corrections until the dog will do a command, which can result in a hysterical dog that is unable to work or, if he finally gets the lesson, might hate his trainer and his lessons.

Most dogs are not basically stubborn about learning. Stubbornness usually occurs after the dog has learned what you want but doesn't feel like doing it. The dog cannot do something he doesn't understand, and many people confuse this with stubbornness; they believe the dog knows what is wanted of him, but the dog actually does not know or has forgotten. A certain amount of pressure often does need to be used in training, but continued severe correction on a dog that is just learning is a terrible mistake and can result in a mental block.

Another common, serious error is when a dog is put on a command (usually when working off leash), breaks command, and starts to walk around. The trainer will frequently give the dog another command, such as "Rex, come!" and then go to the dog and correct it. This is absolutely wrong! If the dog breaks a command, you must *never* give him a different command and then correct him since the broken command will now be forgotten. If the dog receives the erroneous correction, he will immediately think he is being punished for the most recent command. When the dog breaks a command he is on, jerk him back to the spot he left and correct him for the command he broke. If you blurt out a different command when your dog breaks, you must forget the correction. You have made a verbal error and cannot take back your words. Instead, give him a new command and, after he does it, go back to the one he broke and have him repeat it. If he breaks it again, correct him properly.

Any trainer must always remember that training sessions are serious business, and the dog must learn this. Therefore, during the lesson, never play around with the dog. Save the play and games for rest periods or after the lesson. Unless you follow this rule, your dog will not take his training seriously.

Never permit anyone who does not understand the handling of a trained dog to misuse or abuse the commands being taught because this can quickly ruin much of the training the dog has received. When a dog is given a command, he must carry it out. Often, another person will give commands to the dog and then forget about them if he doesn't obey. If the dog is not going to be made to follow a command, the command should never be given. So while the trainer may be doing a good job of training, some other person in contact with the dog may be doing things to interfere with the training.

Be careful not to correct a dog accidentally nor allow the dog to correct himself if the leash becomes caught or entangled. Pay careful attention to the way the leash is handled while training or working the dog on leash. If an erroneous correction occurs when a dog is working on an exercise, the dog will refuse to do that exercise from then on because he previously received a correction on it.

Another common mistake occurs when the trainer forgets the command he gave the dog. When working a dog, the trainer must concentrate on what he is doing and pay attention not only to the dog but to himself. Dogs are frequently corrected when they shouldn't be or corrected for the wrong thing because of this. If you forget or are not absolutely certain what command you gave the dog, do not correct him. Instead, give the dog another command, then keep your mind on what you are doing.

Training Tips

If you want to train a dog quickly, you can't spend months playing guessing games with him. You have to get right to the point so he knows exactly what he has to do and then you must make him do it.

A dog will not learn to do anything unless he can be corrected to make him do it. A dog is very independent. If he knows what you want and feels like doing it, he'll do it. But if he doesn't feel like it, forget it—unless you train him. A dog really enjoys his own special brand of fun, and he has a lot of energy. But when it comes to doing something he doesn't think is any fun, he simply won't do it.

It takes training for a dog to learn to respect your authority. Although your dog won't consider his training as much fun as chasing a cat, if you handle him right he will learn to enjoy it. You have to maintain the attention, cooperation, and confidence of the dog to train him well and quickly. If you are too easy with him, you won't secure his attention or cooperation. If you are continually too hard on him, you will lose his confidence. To accomplish this, you have to sweeten the bitter. The more corrections a dog must receive or the harder the correction required to obtain his obedience, the more enthusiasm and time you must spend on petting and praising him when he responds correctly and the more enjoyable his play periods must be.

Most people tend to undercorrect or overcorrect their dogs. When a dog is first learning an exercise, best results can usually be obtained by applying three or four repeated corrections, beginning gently and progressively increasing the intensity until the dog responds. After a dog has worked on a particular exercise for three or four days, he should know it well enough to do it. When he refuses to obey or breaks the command, his punishment must increase in severity until he obeys. When a dog repeatedly disobeys a particular command after he knows it, he deserves a firm correction every time he disobeys. He will finally decide he prefers to obey rather than take the correction.

A dog can take a firmer correction than most people think. Proper correction is the minimum degree of punishment required to secure obedience from the dog. Some dogs require firmer correction than others. Once the dog has been well trained and knows his exercises and you have taught him through punishment that he must obey, his obedience becomes a habit and he seldom requires correction.

Dogs that have had a lot of leash work or that have been kept tied up develop powerful neck muscles and tough skin, and that makes them much more unresponsive to corrections. Consequently, a great deal more effort must be used to firmly correct such dogs. This adds to the trainer's work, particularly with large dogs.

When training the dog, petting and praising must always outweigh the correction. While a dog is learning, he will have many corrections. To offset the punishment, spend several seconds to a minute or more petting and praising him after each command. A dog learns through being shown what is wanted of him in a manner he can understand, through repetition, and through the use of praise and correction. The success of the trainer depends on his ability to secure the best possible use of these elements.

Also concentrate on what you are doing and apply yourself with sincerity. Develop a good working relationship with your dog and gain his confidence. You can accomplish this by talking soothingly and pleasantly to him and by praising and petting him with enthusiasm when he obeys. In addition, you must also develop a dog/master relationship. This means being firm with him and insisting on obedience. You want your word to be law with him; if it isn't he won't pay attention to you.

When training, do not work too long on a single command. Repetition of one exercise bores a dog until he is only halfway paying attention. I usually work a dog for 10 to 15 minutes on a command and then go to another one. Later, I will repeat them again. Give the dog a 10-minute rest period every 30 or 45 minutes. To train him well and quickly, you have to keep his attention and his interest. Lessons should last about 1 hour to 1½ hours. Or you can have two 1-hour sessions per day. The more practice a dog gets, the faster he learns his exercises and the better he performs them. Just don't tire him out by working too long at a time.

Always spend at least 10 minutes after every lesson playing with your dog or even just sitting, petting, and talking to him. Feed him a little meat or something he really likes. I always have at least a half pound of fresh, raw ground beef for my dogs and feed half of it during the recess, a small ball of it at a time, and the remainder after the lesson.

Don't feed your dog before his lesson. A dog should not be worked on a full stomach; some dogs will vomit from the stress of the lesson. They will also appreciate their training treat a great deal more than if they are full.

Some trainers keep a dog locked up and miserable before his lesson and ignore him after it, believing misery beforehand will make the training session more enjoyable. I have the opposite view. I believe in making the dog's recess, snacks, and play as enjoyable as possible. The dog will look forward to his lessons. You want your dog to enjoy his work as much as possible. If he has something to look forward to, the work doesn't seem to be as hard and he will be more willing to cooperate. Some good food and a little fun are the closest things to heaven in the dog's mind.

Other training tips make the job easier. During summer, don't attempt to work your dog during the heat of the day. He will be lazy from the heat and won't make much of an effort to learn or carry out commands. When training the dog, wear soft-type shoes, such as tennis shoes, so you don't hurt him if you accidentally kick him or step on his foot. Above all, make certain your dog is healthy. Don't attempt to make a dog work that is sick, limping, or distraught. It's unfair and you won't get good results.

The training should be done in an enclosed area until the dog is working well off leash and particularly so if you are training a dog that belongs to someone else. If you are in a populated area where there is traffic, there is danger of the dog being hit by a car if he should run off. A fenced backyard is ideal. Don't work your dog on a paved area. If you put him down too hard, he could be hurt or bite his tongue. In addition, you might trip over the dog when working him and could hurt yourself on the pavement. A lawn is the best place to work your dog.

Until the dog is working quite well, you should not have any distractions around during the lesson. Keep the kids or other dogs out of the way. You can't concentrate and neither can the dog when there are disturbances and distracting activities in the training area. Once the dog is trained, distractions should be added, but not while he is learning. They will only serve to interfere with the progress of the training. If someone must watch you, they should sit quietly off at the sidelines so you will have the dog's undivided attention. Your dog isn't going to learn anything if you can't keep his mind on you.

During the early stages of the training, it is best for only one person to work the dog. Frequently, two people will not work the dog in the same way and this can confuse him. Once his training has been completed, let other members of the family work the dog, so he will learn that he must obey them too. However, they must be taught to do it *correctly*. When another person begins to work the dog, the leash should be put on and the dog should do his commands, giving corrections when needed. Then the leash can be taken off, and the dog will work for this person. Most dogs will not work well, if at all, for anyone who has not worked with them previously. To avoid making your dog a slow worker, move quickly through his commands and exercises.

During the training, do a lot of talking to your dog. As the training reaches the final stages, you can gradually reduce the amount of talking.

When the training is completely finished, it is not actually necessary to talk to the dog, except when praising or giving commands.

This training course teaches the dog both verbal and hand commands at the same time. During the first 10 days or so of the training, both hand and verbal commands should be used at the same time, unless otherwise specified. As the dog begins to learn his commands, he will also be practiced on both types of commands separately. In addition, the dog will not be trained in any set pattern. The commands and exercises should be varied so as not to get the dog in the habit of doing them in any particular order. A dog quickly becomes a creature of habit if he is worked in any set routine, and you want to avoid this so he will respond to whatever command you give, whenever you give it.

As I mentioned earlier, you can begin training a dog as young as 4 months of age. Pups that are being trained must be handled much more gently than what is normally necessary for older dogs because they become upset more easily and you can make them afraid if you are too rough with them. Also, their bones are soft and more easily injured.

The older the dog you are training, the more habits he has acquired; the longer these habits have existed, the more difficult it is to change them. This means spending more time working the dog on his commands and getting him to abandon old habits. If a dog has a long-standing habit of doing something wrong, he is going to be more persistent about holding on to that habit than if he had never learned it. For example, a young intelligent dog that has seldom been on a leash can be taught to heel in about a half hour. However, another dog with the same degree of intelligence that has been dragging you down the street for the past year is going to want to continue dragging you. So it is going to take more practice and more correcting to break that habit before he will begin making an effort to learn a new habit of heeling properly.

The easiest dogs to train are those from a kennel or those that have only been fed and petted, have not been abused, or have not undergone improper attempts to train them. Bad habits develop most frequently through the everyday contact with people who do not know how to properly handle or discipline the dog.

Never permit your dog to disobey a command at any time. If you don't intend to enforce a command, don't give it. Even after a dog is trained, it doesn't take much for him to get back into the habit of disobedience.

Don't ever call a dog to you to correct him; go get him. Any time your dog requires disciplinary action, you must go to him to mete out your punishment. If you call a dog and then punish him, you are breaking him of obeying your command to come.

Reactions of Dogs to Training

No two dogs think alike, and because they don't think alike, they don't act alike. When you start training your dog, you may encounter several different reactions from the dog that you probably didn't expect. Every dog has a reason for the things he does, and since this has an effect on the training, you must understand these actions and know how to cope with them.

Dog Runs or Hides

Many dogs will run or hide at the start of the second or third lesson. He sees you coming with his training leash, and realizing that a lesson is coming, he wants to avoid it if he can. This is your signal to make the recess and the postlesson play and petting more enjoyable for your dog. Feed him some meat or something he really likes when you stop working him. Dogs remember something they liked better than something they didn't like if the pleasure was enough to offset the unpleasantness. If a dog continues to run or hide, even after the third or fourth lesson, you have worked him too long at a time, have been too rough on him, didn't spend enough time petting and praising him after each exercise, or didn't make his rest periods enjoyable. Stop and re-evaluate your methods to find out what you have been doing wrong. You want your dog to enjoy his training, not hate it.

Dog Does Not Pay Attention

Some dogs are much more easily distracted than others. Until the dog has learned all his commands and exercises, there should be no distracting influences in the training area. It is very difficult to train a dog that is being distracted by other dogs running around or children playing nearby. If you can't keep his mind and attention on you, how can you teach him anything?

If your dog is so easily distracted that he watches the birds and the bees and anything else he can think of, you have to do something about it. The way you handle this situation depends on how far along you are in the training. Some dogs will act this way because their minds tend to wander. Other dogs will do it because they don't want to work. Like an ostrich that sticks its head in the sand, dogs think that if they pretend you aren't there, you might take your training leash and go away. If this happens during the first few days of training, don't worry about it as long as the dog obeys the command you have given him. If the dog continues to ignore you, as a stall on obeying a command, then quickly sneak up on him and give him a good correction for the command he didn't obey. Correct him every time he ignores you.

If the dog has had several days of training and is still ignoring you, give him a hand command as you stand in front of him. If he doesn't immediately obey the hand command (for sit or down), quickly give him a correction for that command. Some dogs are smart enough that even though they may be looking off in another direction, they will watch you out of the corner of their eye. When they see that hand command, they will obey it. You can't correct the dog just because he isn't looking at you. But you *can* correct him if you give him a command and he doesn't obey it. If you are working the dog off leash and he begins ignoring you, give him a hand command when he isn't looking at you. Be sure to do so within 6 to 8 feet of the dog. Have the leash rolled up in your hand to be prepared for him to ignore you and not obey the command. Then quickly throw the rolled up leash at him. Take care not to hit him in the face, however. The instant he turns to look at you in surprise, quickly give him the hand (and oral) command again. If he doesn't do it, immediately go and correct him as you repeat the command.

Dog Looks Away, Lays Ears Back, or Lies Down

When a dog does this, he has either received too many corrections within a short period or has been corrected too hard. Because he has been overcorrected, he is worrying about getting another correction and is unable to concentrate on the command. When this happens, go up to your dog and talk to him. Show him what you want, by gently placing him in the position of the command given as you repeatedly say the command in a more gentle tone of voice. Then pet and praise him, take him off command, and play with him for a little while. This helps to clear his mind and makes him forget about the corrections that worried him.

Dog Quickly Turns Head From Side to Side, Fidgets, or Whines

When a dog does this, he doesn't understand what you want him to do. Do not correct him or you will confuse him further and upset him. Instead, show him what you want him to do by gently putting him in proper position for the command given. For example, if the command was Down, gently pull him down and at the same time say the command two or three times. When he is in position, pet and praise him with a lot of joy. After several days of training, a dog usually knows all his commands quite well but sometimes may not recall one at the moment.

Dog Cries or Lets Out a Yelp When He Makes a Mistake

The dog may perform a command wrong and then let out a yelp or cry. He does this because he either was not paying full attention to the command or temporarily forgot the command and realizes that he has done it wrong and will be corrected. When this happens, instead of correcting the dog, repeat the command and give him a chance to do it right. If he does it correctly this time, pet and praise him and don't be stingy with your praise.

Dog Won't Do a Command He Knows or Does Wrong Command

Excluding a mental block (discussed in Chapter 1), confusion will cause a dog to disobey or wrongly perform a given command. A new command he has been learning recently may have bewildered and confused him about a previous command. Sometimes a dog may respond by refusing to do it or more often will do the wrong command. When this happens, work the dog on that command at the end of the lesson, until he finally does it. Then pet and praise him joyfully and end the lesson. (It is preferable to do this in the evening.) Don't play with him after this lesson. Instead, put him wherever he is normally kept for the night. Don't permit anyone to play with him. Let him sleep on that command. The next day, make this command the *first* one you give him. The dog will usually perform it with little or no hesitation.

Dog Cowers or Crawls and Whines

When a dog cowers (shrinks his head and body toward the ground), he is pain sensitive or your corrections have simply been too much for him. These dogs need a lot of praise and petting, and you must be a little easier on most of your corrections.

Dog Growls, Snaps, or Tries to Bite

Dogs react this way because they don't like your corrections. The situation can be handled in several different ways, depending on what the dog does.

Personally, I never punish a dog for biting. If the dog is being used as a watch dog or is going to be trained later for guard work, I certainly don't want to ruin him by correcting him for biting. If a dog is very aggressive, a "get tough" attitude on the part of the trainer who might be working a strange dog is likely to result in making the dog more hostile.

When training begins, some dogs will get hostile when they find their activities are suddenly restricted and they cannot get away from you. Some may growl, snap, or nip at the toe of your shoe, the leash, or even your hand or leg. Others will simply try to bite you.

When teaching the heeling exercise, some dogs will bite at the leash. The dog figures it is hurting him, and he attempts to stop it by biting the leash. The dog that bites at your hand is usually smarter. He knows your hand is pulling the leash that hurts him, so he attempts to correct that by getting right to the source. When a dog begins nipping or snapping at you, promptly give him the command to heel and give him a quick, short jerk with the leash to make him come along at heeling position. After you have given him the command and correction, walk only a few feet and stop. Make him sit next to you and quickly begin petting and praising him and talking to him for at least 2 or 3 minutes to calm him down. Then begin heeling him again, but ease up on your corrections—you may be correcting him too hard.

If the dog continues to try to bite you after you begin heeling him again (even after reducing the intensity of your corrections and spending more time petting and praising him), correct him this way. As he attempts to nip, again repeat the heel command and, at the same time, jerk him in toward your left leg and give him your knee in his face. Then pull him next to your left side (at heel position) and make him sit. Then pet and praise him. Usually, one knee correction (two at the most) is enough to put a stop to the biting.

If you are working with a dog that shows his teeth and seriously tries to get in a good bite, quickly put one foot on top of the leash (holding it to the ground) and forcefully pull the end of the leash with both hands to make it slide quickly under your shoe all the way to the dog's chin, forcing the dog's head to the ground. Immediately begin talking to the dog in a soothing voice and rubbing him on the side of his body with one hand as you hold the leash with the other hand. Hold the pressure on the leash for only about 30 seconds and then loosen it slightly so the dog is not being choked but is still held to the ground. Continue talking to him and petting him for several minutes, until he calms down. Then let him up.

A shy or timid dog, under stress, is even more likely to bite than an aggressive dog. However, these dogs must be handled entirely differently. They will usually try to get as far away from you as the leash will permit. If a dog that is afraid begins growling, showing signs of biting you, and you attempt to jerk him toward you, he may immediately start chewing on you. So you must use a different approach. Immediately begin talking to the dog in a soothing voice as you slowly walk toward him, reeling in the leash as you walk. But do not pull or jerk on him. Keep talking to him as you slowly maneuver next to the dog's right side. Then begin gently scratching his neck and talking to him for several minutes until he calms down to where you can begin working with him again. This type of dog is neurotic, emotional, and often unpredictable, but if you have the desire, patience, and time to train him, it can be done. However the final results are never as satisfying as with a mentally stable dog.

Always use caution when petting a strange dog or one that may be inclined to bite. Do not put your face close to the dog. When you pet him, hold the leash in your right hand and scratch his chest with the same hand. At the same time, hold your left forearm near the right side of the dog's head. You can then protect your face if he attempts to bite you, by knocking his muzzle aside. I always keep one foot on the leash while petting such dogs to be prepared to quickly stand up and pull the leash under my shoe and force their head against the ground if they decide to bite. You have to be prepared with these dogs since you won't have much time to act.

Some dogs may bite if you try to correct them after letting them get by with disobedience for awhile. Then you really have a problem. The dog is going to try to train you instead of you training him. You cannot back down from correcting him for disobedience, even if he threatens you. If you do, he knows he has won and will dominate you from then on.

The over-indulged, spoiled dog may also nip you when you finally decide to train him. Unlike the dog that is neglected, abused, or emotionally starved for attention and affection and whose main contacts with his owner have been unpleasant, the spoiled dog will not usually become hostile, though he may sulk over corrections. The spoiled dog is like a sassy child, accustomed to having his own way, and rejects the idea of you wanting to change things to make him do what you want. He wants life to remain the way it is. When you begin correcting him to make him stay, lie down, and so forth, he doesn't want to do it. He wants to be near you or jump on you to secure your constant petting and attention. He dislikes being corrected to make him do things he doesn't want to do. So he may nip you when you correct him to discourage you from forcing him to do something you want. As your corrections get harder, so may his bites. He still wants your affection, but he also wants to continue having your indulgence and to dominate you. He prefers being served rather than being the servant. He doesn't want to loose his previous status and the freedom it allowed or to give way to your sudden new demands.

I dislike punishing a dog for biting because some dogs tend to be useless afterwards for any type of guard work. Other dogs, if you start beating them, will become mean. If you hit him with a stick or piece of hose, you are challenging him to a fight and are teaching him your strategy. The next time he decides to nip you, he will be prepared to outmaneuver you to defend himself and still get the best of you. You don't want to challenge the dog to a duel, which you are doing if you try a mutual combat maneuver. If you whip a dog for nipping, you are challenging him to a battle. He may take you up on it and turn hostile toward you. You want to teach him to obey you, so you can't be afraid of him. You have to correct him for the command you gave him and make him do it.

If a dog I am training nips me when I attempt to correct him, I give him a terrific correction for the command he didn't do. Then I put the leash on him and work him on the Heel, Sit, and Down commands for about 10 minutes, giving him a terrific correction the same time, or an instant after, I give each command. I orally praise him after he does each command, but do not pet him. When I have finished, I take him off command, pet him, and give him a little meat to show him there are no hard feelings. Then I tie him to something and don't work him for about another half hour. Every time he nips when I correct him, I do the same thing. This impresses on a dog that if he nips you for correcting him, you are going to correct him anyway and work him that much rougher. After you have done this routine a few times, the dog will realize that the nipping did not stop his training, in fact, it made his treatment more harsh. Moreover, he is still being punished for disobeying commands.

Every dog prefers his freedom rather than having to obey your commands. And at the same time, they don't like being corrected to make them do something they don't want to do. So they usually attempt to get out of it by running off or biting. Some dogs are unbelievably persistent at attempting to get the best of you and training them requires your unlimited perseverance.

If your dog challenges you, for any reason, there are only two things you can do—fight it out with him or use reverse psychology. It isn't the best idea in the world to attempt to fight it out because when a dog challenges you, he is generally prepared to fight. His adrenalin is already built up. If you try whipping him, you are only going to provoke him further and future encounters are very likely.

When a dog challenges you, it's for one reason—he has no use for you. Your previous relationship with him has undoubtedly been a poor one. You probably showed him no interest, attention, or affection, and he has responded by disliking you.

Reverse psychology is the best course to follow. You must brainwash the dog and change his attitude toward you. This can easily be done. Instead of trying to retaliate against him, be nice to him. Talk to him in a soothing voice, offer him some meat and pet him. If you are trying to train him, halt the training until you are able to establish a more companionable relationship with your dog. If you make the effort, you can accomplish this in a couple of weeks.

You can always tell what sort of a relationship a person has with their dog just from watching them and their dog at home. If the dog strays off by himself, the relationship is not good. But, if the dog follows his owners around and sits by them, you know they give their dog attention and love.

The Hard Head

The hard-headed dog is sometimes thought to be dumb. This is not always true. He can simply be very obstinate about doing something he doesn't want to do. Most people tend to give up on these dogs because they think it's a hopeless case, whether they believe it is a result of stupidity or stubbornness. Not many dogs are this way, but those that are can really be a problem for their owner. But they can be trained and generally will work almost as well (and sometimes better) as any other dog.

If you have worked the dog repeatedly for a few days on a command and properly shown him what is expected of him through light to gradually increasing firmer corrections, praised him enthusiastically when he was made to do it, and still are not able to get him to perform that command, you may have one of these dogs. He may be stubborn about one command or several, particularly when you are away from his side. They will usually obey when you are right next to them.

Sometimes these dogs will look straight at you when you give them a command but refuse to do it. They may turn their head slightly while you correct them and look at you out of the corner of their eye, or they may run off at every opportunity. If the dog is performing the command when you are next to him, you know that he knows it and it's time to make him do it. These dogs can often take a harsher correction than you may be able to give, but give it everything you've got, every time they refuse to obey. It may take you a few days of some harsh correcting on the command he won't do, but you will finally convince him. Once he learns he has to knuckle down, he will do it, and you probably won't have any more trouble with him.

A dog that has an obstinate nature is one that should never be permitted to be disobedient on commands—not even one time. If you fail to correct him a few times, he will begin refusing to obey all over again and it may take some severe correcting to get him back in line.

You have to do a lot of praising with these dogs when you do get them to obey. Since they do need more correcting, you must give them lots of praise or they can easily get the idea you are being hostile toward them. You never want a dog to start thinking that way or he may turn hostile toward you.

The 14-Day Dog Training Method

Standard obedience courses are divided into three groups that could be classified as elementary school, high school, and junior college. They are called novice, open, and utility. Novice (basic) obedience training generally requires 10 to 12 weeks of daily training. The intermediate and advanced courses require 4 months each.

The obedience method I developed consists of all novice training and parts of open and utility, plus some extra exercises not taught in regular obedience work. This course is designed particularly for the working dog, the family dog, and the dog destined for specialized training. I have selected all the most important exercises needed for advanced types of work as well as those most commonly needed and used every day around the home. This 2-week course consists of teaching the dog the following commands and exercises.

Heel The dog walks at your left side when you are walking. When you stop walking, the dog automatically sits at your left side.

Stay The dog stays while you walk away when you give a hand or voice command. The dog also stays at a distance on hand or voice commands.

Down The dog lies down when you give a voice or hand command, regardless of where you are standing.

Sit The dog sits when you give a hand or voice command, regardless of where you are standing.

Come (recall) The dog comes to you and sits in front of you when you give a hand or voice command.

Finish The dog returns to heel position and sits, ready for you to walk away.

Stand The dog goes to a standing position from a sit or down position, on a hand or voice command, without you going near or putting your hands on him.

Motion exercises The dog performs and obeys commands when he is moving, either walking or running, toward you or away from you. For example, you can call the dog to you and while he is coming, you can give him a command to stay, sit, or lie down and he will obey.

Off leash The dog performs all commands and exercises without being on leash.

Perfect sits The dog sits straight, in correct position, on the automatic sit at heel position and also on the recall.

Distraction work The dog performs his commands and exercises in spite of anything that would normally distract him or cause him to disobey.

This training method has been engineered in such a manner that it is possible to compress months of training into 2 weeks and yet have a more proficient dog than is generally possible with older training methods. This is possible because of the use of a combination of factors and techniques that enables the dog to understand and learn more quickly and efficiently. Each command is taught to the dog in such a manner that he is able to learn it thoroughly and independently. Because the training progresses so rapidly, there are changes in the process from day to day. I have therefore described it in day by day lessons to simplify it for you. Each day, the dog learns a new command or new exercise. A very intelligent dog is able to learn more than one exercise per day but the training would be so fast-paced that an inexperienced person might have difficulty performing it.

I have also included a chapter on the various types of problems people often encounter when training a dog on various exercises. This chapter explains how to correct these problems quickly and easily. Quite often, the problems people have in training a dog are a result of mistakes they made. But if a person is not aware of what he has been doing wrong, it is impossible to correct it. Many people are interested in obedience competition, but most are not particularly successful. Many dogs that have the potential to be good working dogs never make the grade because the person training them makes too many mistakes in performing the training or simply doesn't know how to correct the problems he may encounter in teaching his particular dog.

It is entirely possible to train a dog to perform with precision. However, the trainer must also be precise in his work with the dog to accomplish this.

One of the biggest weaknesses of usual obedience training methods is control, which has long been admitted by dog trainers. While the training was usually effective, it still did not provide the desired control under uncontrollable conditions. It did not stop a dog from chasing a cat in front of a speeding automobile; it did not prevent or break up a dog fight; it did not stop a dog determined to chase and bite someone; it did not keep a dog from running away if he wanted to do so.

My training methods have been able to overcome all these problems with control, because the dog is precision trained. I admit that many trainers are astounded at the results I have attained. The sentry dog trainers at Norton Air Force Base in California were quite stunned at the control and precision work of my attack dogs. But why have a poorly trained dog if you can have a well-trained dog? You can also teach your dog to be precise in his work if you make the effort to be precise in your training.

While absolute control has seldom been previously attainable in most training procedures, the reason for this has never been clearly known. If so, it could have been corrected. Actually, there are several reasons why trainers have failed to attain control. The dog has not generally been trained in a manner that enables him to understand his commands completely; work with distractions is not fully understood and put to proper use; and sometimes corrections are not firm enough at the proper time. There is a time to be firm and a time to be gentle. Yet, firm corrections still will not produce the desired results unless the dog understands his commands clearly. In addition, the dog has to be trained with the proper *types* of distractions to get the right effect. Total control over a dog is three sided. The first is *command understanding;* the second is the *right type of distractions;* and the third is *proper correction.* At the end of 14 days, you will know what to do to accomplish total control.

In this training, I use a different correction for each command. Each correction is quite precise, so you must not use the wrong correction for a particular command. By using a different correction for each command, it enables the dog to learn the correction as well as the command and he correlates one with the other. If he forgets a command, the correction tells him what it was.

Thousands of people in this world don't know anything about dog training. Yet, they love dogs and are able to establish communication with the dog to a limited extent, especially with puppies. Many people come to my kennel and bring their children. As a rule, the adults will sit and talk, but the children want to play with the puppies. If you have ever noticed, children will call a puppy with their voices and also with their hands. Some will clap their hands; some will sit on the ground and pat the ground to draw the pup's attention. Some will click their fingers, pretending they have something in their hand for the puppy to eat. Even children know the puppy can't understand what they want, until they start using their hands.

One of the fastest ways of training dogs is by showing them what you want them to do by using your hands. You can sit on the ground and tap the ground with your hand, and the puppy will come to you. When you start petting the pup, he will lie down so he can be petted some more. When you get up, he will also get up because he's watching the movement of your body. If you start patting your leg with your hand, as a rule, the pup will jump up on your leg so he can be petted. He knows your hand is a comfort to him.

When working with a puppy or a dog, you should always start with a sign language as well as with your voice. Most trainers do their training by using their voice and corrections. The dog cannot understand our words, and the training is made much more difficult for him. A person automatically uses sign language with another person who cannot speak their language.

It is no different when training dogs. A dog will pick up sign language much faster than voice commands. This is one method of training dogs quickly. So be sure to always give the hand command with the voice command.

If a dog is completely trained with hand and voice commands in English, it will make no difference what language a person speaks. By using the hand commands with their language, the dog will understand their oral command words in less than a week and very little correcting will be necessary.

Dogs will easily learn to check out things to which you point. They don't know what you want them to do unless you teach them, but they quickly catch on that you want them to go to the object or spot to which you are pointing.

If your dog gets hurt or frightened, he will run to you seeking your pity and consolation. If you accidentally step on your dog's foot and hurt him, he'll yelp and look at you momentarily to see what your reaction is going to be. You should quickly say, "Oh you poor dog! I didn't mean to hurt you. Let me see your foot." Your dog doesn't understand a word you're saying, but he knows from your tone of voice and actions that you are sorry and want to comfort him. And he'll quickly forgive you.

But if you hurt him and then ignore him, he feels dejected and abused. If you repeatedly hurt or punish him and then ignore him, the dog believes you have a grudge against him. He is either going to become afraid of you or develop a dislike for you. Either way, he won't want anything to do with you. The only thing he'll learn from your abuse is that you are a mean person.

Corrections are definitely required to teach a dog to obey commands. But for a dog to understand *why* he is being punished, a correction must also *show* him what he must do. Another important point is that the more frequent or the harder the correction that is required to get a dog to obey, the more time and effort you must spend each time you praise him or the bigger the fuss you must make over him. Talk soothingly to him when you are working with him. This is absolutely necessary to make the dog realize your punishment is intended *only* to make him obey your commands and *not* because you dislike him. You have to make every effort to thoroughly convince the dog of this fact and then *keep him convinced*. When a dog has to be frequently corrected, he is inclined to be suspicious that you have an ulterior motive for punishing him.

To train a dog well, you must be firm and insist on his obedience to every command. But you must also continually prove to him that your punishment does not lean toward ill will or spite on your part. If you fail to do this, a dog will relate your punishment to bad personal feelings instead of the command you gave him. He may begin to dislike you and won't want to cooperate because he will lose confidence in you.

It requires *both* affection and discipline to produce a superiorly trained dog that is not only obedient but cooperative and willing. There will also be a tremendous improvement in his personality.

People who have watched trained dog demonstrations or obedience trials believe that the dogs are able to perform any variation of the actual command or exercises they see. But this is not true. For example, in the retrieving exercise called the "scent discrimination exercise" that is taught in advanced obedience training, a dog is sent out a few feet from his owner to retrieve a small dumbbell laying amongst several other dumbbells. He is supposed to fetch the dumbbell that has his owner's scent. Most people (even many training their dog) believe this is scent training and the dog would also be able to retrieve any type of item, containing whatever scent they give the dog. But this is a false impression. The dog can only do exactly what he was trained to do. The only variations he can perform are limited to those he has been taught.

Something else most people do not know about dog training is that a dog can be trained to obey or perform certain commands when you are close to him, but he will not usually obey these same commands when you are farther away from him. Therefore, once he has learned to obey particular commands when you are near him, he must then be taught to obey them when you are farther away. Even after he learns this, he still will not necessarily obey a command given when he is *moving* (walking or running toward you or away from you). So he must also be taught to obey commands given when he is moving, which I call "motion exercises." For example, you can teach a dog to lie down near you and even to remain down while you walk away. But if he is standing or sitting 50 feet away from you and you command him to lie down, he very likely will not do it. He is more likely to walk away or come to you. He may just simply ignore you. This might seem strange to you because most people think that once a dog learns a command, he should perform it at any time, regardless of where he is or what he is doing. But this is not so. The dog only learns to do something *exactly the way he is taught* and nothing more.

Proper Use of Corrections

When a dog is learning a new command or exercise, corrections should generally be as mild as possible so they serve the purpose of *showing* the dog what he must do rather than acting as a punishment. This can best be done

Training Commands

Verbal command*	Hand command†	Exercise
Heel (Forward)	Snap fingers (of left hand held down at your side) or Wave forward (with open left hand down at side)	Dog walks forward at your left side
Heel (Finish)	Open right hand, motion (wave) toward your rear	Command given when dog is sitting in front of and facing you; dog goes around your right side and behind you to sit on your left
Sit	Open right hand held down at your side, then raised forward and upward (palm UP)	Dog sits
Down	Open right hand, raised above your head and then lowered downward (palm DOWN)	Dog lies down
Come	Stand erect; point to your feet with right forefinger	Dog comes to you and sits in front of you, or dog comes to your left side if you start walking AWAY from him
Stay	Given at dog's side: open left hand (palm toward dog) passed 6 inches in front of dog's nose Given away from dog: open right hand (palm toward dog) extended toward dog, making a "pushing" motion	Dog stays where he is
Stand	Open right hand (palm UP), motion from right to left just in front of your waist (as if to "slice" the air with the edge of your hand)	Dog stands on all four feet
Okay	Raise both hands in the air in a "V" for victory type motion	Dog is released from command

*Dog's name precedes every verbal command given.
†Each hand command consists of a single motion with the hand, which may be repeated if desired.

by giving two or three consecutive mild corrections rather than one hard one. However, any time proper correction *repeatedly* applied on any exercise does not produce results with a dog, the correction must get firm enough until the dog will do the command or exercise. The instant the dog responds to the correction, he should be praised immediately.

I will never quit on an exercise until the dog does it. The more times he does it, the better he gets at doing it. However, I also do not keep drilling a dog for more than about 20 minutes at a time on one exercise. If he is sloppy

Basic Corrections for Each Command

Command	Correction
Heel (Forward)	Straight forward jerk on leash in the direction you are walking.
Heel (Finish)	Short jerks on leash toward your right rear. When dog gets to your rear, tap him on the rump with the heel of your right foot and pull him to your left side. Then make him sit at your left side.
Sit	*Dog standing*—Leash jerked at a 45-degree angle, toward rear of dog. *Dog lying down*—Leash jerked straight up.
Down	Leash held so slack droops 4 to 12 inches above ground (distance depending on size of dog; close to ground for very small dogs). Place one foot on drooping part of leash and press leash to ground with your foot.
Come	*On leash*—Short jerks on leash toward you. *Off Leash*—Go to dog and attach leash. Taking dog with you, run back to the same spot you had stood when giving the command to come, applying three jerks forward with the leash as you run. With each jerk, firmly repeat the come command. Put dog in sitting position in front of you. Make sure you and dog are facing the same directions you were when the command was given. (You and dog should be facing each other.)
Stay	Short, sharp, horizontal jerk on leash toward rear of dog.
Stand	Place foot under dog's belly, raising dog to standing position and apply short jerks forward (at a slightly upward angle) with leash.

at performing it, I will quit after he finally does it reasonably well at least one time and then work on something else before trying that exercise again. After a dog has been worked a couple of days on a command or exercise and has to be corrected three or four times in a row on that command or exercise, I will generally give him a firm correction that he will remember for awhile.

I like to minimize the correcting on the heeling exercise as much as possible for the first few days since it is a simple exercise and I prefer not to upset the dog with too much or too hard correcting on it. The other exercises often require firmer correction, so I try to reduce the amount of correcting on the heeling.

Corrections must be properly applied to serve their best use as well as be humane. Most people tend to give long, torturous corrections even though they produce few results. Even though the choke collar is called a "choke," its purpose is not intended for a slow strangulation of the dog.

The proper correction consists of a *fast*, sharp jerk on the leash that is slackened as quickly as it is applied. The more slack used and the harder the jerk, the firmer the correction. Correction must be done *quickly*. Do not *pull* on the leash—*jerk* it and quickly slacken it. The faster you can snap the leash, the better. The intensity of your corrections should always correspond to the size of your dog as well as the occasion. The best corrections are those that can be completed in a split second.

The choke collar must always be loosened before the start of an exercise and can be done when petting the dog. If the choke collar is not loose, you will *not* get a proper correction. It will be a "choke" instead of a sudden jerk. The loosening of the choke collar is like setting a trap. It must be ready to go off when you need it. Test this on your arm and you will see the difference. Tighten the choke collar on your arm and jerk it. Then loosen it and jerk it again and you will understand what I mean.

Two very common mistakes people make on corrections are giving the *wrong correction* for a command broken or disobeyed or giving an accidental correction when a dog *is performing* an exercise. These mistakes can really disrupt the training.

But some people think that because it takes so much correcting to teach a dog to perform a command one little correction mistake couldn't possibly make any difference. WRONG! One little mistake can ruin all the work you have already done on that command. Avoiding such mistakes is one of the secrets of training a dog to do precision work and of training a dog quickly. It may take many corrections to teach a dog to perform a command, but it only takes one good wrong one to *break* him of performing that command.

When a dog is being trained, he must always be able to clearly identify the correction with the command for which he is being punished. Anytime he is corrected in such a manner that he relates that correction to a *different* command, he will begin refusing to do that other command, which can easily occur once the dog begins learning his commands.

I have been watching dog show obedience enthusiasts working their dogs for many years. The numerous performance problems they have with their dogs are almost unbelievable to me. Some of these dogs have been in daily training for as long as 4 years! But what these people don't seem to realize is that most of their problems stem from the mistakes they make or have made earlier in the training. Most people don't seem to know there is such a thing as trainer error. They believe the only dummy in the place is their dog and never dream they could be doing anything wrong.

Corrections are normally considered, classified, and used strictly for the purpose of punishment in dog training. Most people use fewer types of corrections and practically the same degree of correction intensity throughout the training, beginning with the first lesson. Corrections that do not show a dog what to do or that are too severe before a dog understands what is wanted of him drastically hinder the training process.

When teaching a dog an exercise (or a variation of an exercise), corrections for the first several days should usually be mild, using just enough force to get the dog to do it (so he knows what you want) and yet not hurt him. However, if a particular dog is extremely resistant and determined not to comply, his correction must gradually get firmer until he will comply. The corrections in my training methods are designed to serve three purposes: (1) they show the dog what to do, (2) they assist the dog to do what is wanted, and (3) they also serve as punishment once the dog knows how to do a command but refuses to do it.

TEN RULES FOR SUCCESSFUL TRAINING

1 Give oral commands loud and clear; give hand commands distinctly.

2 Repeat commands (hand and oral) *often* while the dog is learning.

3 Talk to the dog in a soothing, happy voice most of the time during lessons. This helps to keep his mind on you and lessens the mental stress from corrections because it shows him you are dispassionately, and without rancor, correcting him *only* for disobedience not because you have a grudge against him. (Grudges are a very real part of the dog's social world and psychological makeup, and he recognizes and reacts to such behavior.)

4 Always praise enthusiastically to reward him for compliance.

5 Remember to correct *only for the last command given* if the dog disobeys or refuses to obey.

6 Always correct for noncompliance or disobedience to a command. The dog *must do* the command given him.

7 *Repeat* the disobeyed command as you correct.

8 Keep distracting or disturbing influences out of the training area while the dog is learning.

9 Always use the *proper correction* for the command given.

10 Be fair to the dog; praise him when he obeys, correct him when he doesn't. But don't be generally abusive just to prove you are bigger than he is. Such tactics don't produce dependable results nor do they develop a good working relationship.

Lesson 1

Heeling with Automatic Sit Exercise

The first lesson involves teaching the Heeling exercise. Every dog can usually be taught to perform this exercise in a couple of days if the instructions are followed. It is the most simple exercise for the dog to learn and yet requires practice if the dog is to perform it well. I do not attempt to attain perfection right from the beginning. The main object is to teach the dog the exercise so that he knows what is expected of him and yet not upset him with too much correcting on it since he has many other more difficult things to learn. After several days of training, you can gradually and progressively work toward perfection on this exercise.

Initially, there should be little problem with this lesson with dogs that have learned to walk on a leash. However, their bad habits may require a little more time and correcting to break. Those dogs that are not leash trained will present somewhat more of a hectic situation in the beginning and their reactions will vary. Most will attempt to fight the leash and make every effort to get away from you. When this first phase passes, which usually happens after one lesson, they begin learning to heel very quickly.

My training methods are quite different for the most part and often completely opposite from any other methods, which require *much* longer to teach a dog considerably fewer exercises. If you have had some experience at using other methods, do not attempt to mix those procedures with the instructions for this method. For example, some methods advocate teaching a dog the Heeling exercise by giving the dog plenty of loose lead and walking at a very fast pace—forward, left, right, and making fast pivots to go in the opposite direction, repeatedly applying numerous, hard jerks on the leash. It doesn't take the dog long to realize that he is in a "torture chamber," but it does take a great deal of time for him to figure out what he must do to bring about an end to it. But he is so busy thinking about his sore neck that he doesn't have much opportunity to think about anything else.

Instructions for Heeling Exercise

Although this exercise is called Heeling with Automatic Sit, the sit is not "automatic" when the dog is first learning. It becomes automatic as soon as the dog begins to know what he is required to do. The exercise consists of teaching the dog to walk only at your left side, close to but not touching your left leg. The dog is required to stay parallel with you so that his head is just about even with your body at all times, regardless of how fast or slow you are moving. Each time you stop, the dog is supposed to sit at your side, about 6 inches from your left leg and with his front feet about parallel to or slightly behind your toes.

The problems that can occur in teaching this exercise vary from one dog to another. There are a variety of corrections and ways to eliminate these difficulties and thereby teach the dog to perform correctly. Refer to the section at the end of the book for instructions on how to handle your particular dog to teach him the exercise, curb his faults, and correct his mistakes.

To begin the lesson, put the training choke collar on the dog and attach the six-foot leash. Double-check that you have the choke on correctly, as described in Chapter 1. The dog should not have any other collar on his neck except the choke collar that will be used for training. Stand next to the dog, on his right side. Pet him and talk to him for a few seconds.

To begin teaching the exercise, hold the leash in both hands. Grasp the loose end of the leash with the right hand, approximately 18 inches from the end. With your left hand straight down at your side, grasp hold of the leash at a point near the dog so there is only a few inches of slack, but *no tension* on the dog's neck or choke collar. This will enable you to keep the dog close to your left side and yet not have any tension on the leash when the dog is correctly at your side. If the dog pulls ahead or lags behind, any tension on his choke collar will be of his own doing and he quickly realizes this.

You may hold the leash in front of your body, as is usually done in this exercise. However, if the dog is anxious and determined to pull ahead or jerk forward, attempting to go ahead of you, it works best to hold the leash behind your back. This gives you more leverage to hold the dog back as he attempts to pull forward. Even a small dog can display a great deal of strength if he is determined to go in a particular direction.

As soon as you are ready, holding the leash correctly and standing erect at heeling position (at the dog's right side), give the command "Rex, HEEL!" and begin walking forward, stepping out with the left foot first. (To simplify my description of verbal commands, I will use the name of an imaginary dog, but you will use the name of the dog you are training.)

It is never necessary to walk more than 10 or 20 feet for each heel. If a dog is extremely nervous, I will usually walk in a large circle. If the dog is working without too much trouble, select either a large square or rectangular pattern, 20 to 40 feet long.

On the first heeling lesson, it is best not to make any left turns or fast turnabouts. Until the dog begins getting the idea of the whole thing, it works best with most dogs to only make right-hand turns. If a dog is just beginning to learn the exercise, left-hand turns usually involve bumping into him to facilitate the left turn and thereby giving him what he believes to be a correction. Such actions tend to confuse most dogs, making it more difficult for them to understand what is expected of them.

Walk 10 to 20 feet with the dog, trying to keep him near your left side. Talk to the dog as you walk, rotating "Good boy!" with the command. *Always remember, the more often a dog hears (or sees) his command, the faster he will learn it.* Use a happy tone on the praising words and a firm tone when you say the command. If the dog is doing acrobatics as you attempt to walk with him, walk only a few steps at a time, but keep repeating the command as you pull him along with you. Any time he begins coming along with you, even if it is only momentarily, say "Good boy! . . . Rex, HEEL!" If the dog is fighting you, walk more slowly. When he is coming along fairly well, walk at a normal or only slightly faster pace.

After walking a short distance, stop and pull the dog near your left side and say, "Rex, SIT!" as you apply several short jerks on the leash in a slightly upward direction toward the rear of the dog (at a 45-degree angle). Keep repeating the command, "Rex, SIT!" until you get him to sit. As soon as he sits, pet him and give him a lot of praise.

If you cannot get the dog to sit by applying repeated, fast, short jerks on the leash, swing your right foot behind you and tap him on the rump with your toe as you jerk the leash and keep repeating the command (Fig. 1). If it is difficult for you to do it with your right foot, tap the top of his rump with either foot as you jerk the leash. You can also shove his rump down with the left hand if necessary. It usually works best to use your foot so you can jerk the leash at the same time. Keep him sitting while you pet and praise him. If he stands up, repeat the command to sit along with the jerks on the leash and make him sit again. If he should lie down, jerk him up into sitting position. Keep him sitting for about a minute while you pet and praise him. Remember to keep saying the command over and over anytime you are trying to get him to sit. While you are petting him, scratch his neck and loosen his choke collar as you tell him what a good dog he is.

When you have finished praising him, stand erect. Adjust the leash again and check his choke collar to make sure the rings are on the right-hand side of his neck. Do this each time because the choke collar often gets twisted

FIG. 1. The oral command to sit is given as trainer applies jerks at a 45-degree angle toward the dog's rear and pushes dog's rump down, using the instep of right foot.

around on his neck when he is learning. Improper positioning of the choke rings interferes with corrections and slackening of the choke collar and can pinch the skin around the neck as well as get in the way of the dog's face when you are heeling.

Again give the command, "Rex, HEEL!" and walk forward a short distance. When you stop, again pull him next to your left side and command him to sit. Continue repeating the exercise, heel and then sit, heel and sit.

If the dog gets his leg over the top of the leash or gets tangled in it, which he shouldn't if you are holding it properly, stop and straighten it. Don't be rough with the dog when you are getting the leash clear of his legs or body. Then continue with the exercise.

Practice the dog on heeling and sitting for about 1 hour total, but don't work him for that long all at one time. Give him a rest break for about 10 minutes after you have worked him steadily for about 20 minutes. Then work him for another 20 minutes and give him another 10-minute rest. After that, work him for another 20 minutes and then end the lesson for the day. Each time you stop working him and at the end of the lesson, take the dog off command. The off command, which is a command release, will actually be taught to the dog as an exercise.

FIG. 2. The Okay hand command, releasing dog from command.

Off Command

The verbal command for this exercise is "Rex, OKAY!" The hand command is throwing both your arms up in the air in a "V" for victory type motion. Both the verbal and hand commands should be used together.

This command should always be used at any time you end or stop a training session, even for a few minutes, or for a short interruption. There are particular purposes for this command in advanced types of training, but the purpose in obedience work is to teach the dog when he is off command and when he isn't. If you forget to take the dog off command anytime you stop working him, he cannot learn when he is on command and when he is not. The dog will become undependable when he is being worked, particularly when left on a command for a few minutes. He will begin thinking, "Well, nothing seems to be happening, so I guess I can leave." And he will.

To teach this exercise to the dog, while you are standing next to him at heeling position, preparing to end the work session, say "Rex, OKAY!" Pat him on the chest, scratch his neck, and unsnap the leash. Take several steps out in front of him and turn to face him. Throw your arms up in the air and excitedly say, "Rex, OKAY!" (Fig. 2). Repeat this a couple of times. If the dog comes to you, say the command again as you pat and rub him happily. If the dog hesitates to come toward you, walk up to him and pat and rub him, happily saying "Rex, Okay!" When he finally realizes he can run around, let him do so. Pet him and talk to him or play with him for a little while. Feed him a few snacks, such as little balls of raw ground beef. Then let him relax for about 10 minutes. Repeat this procedure each time you stop working him and when you end the lesson for the day.

Lesson 2

Sit/Stay Exercise

Before beginning the second lesson, the choke collar and six-foot training leash should be put on the dog. Pet and talk to the dog in a pleasant voice for several minutes before starting to work him. Each day, practice the previous exercises and then start the new exercise.

Previous Exercise

Do the Heeling with Automatic Sit exercise the same way you did it yesterday. Stand at the dog's right side, which is your heeling position. Hold the leash with both hands with just enough slack between the left hand and the dog so as not to have any tension on the dog's neck, allowing a few inches of slack in the leash. Loosen the choke collar and adjust it so the rings are positioned at the right of the dog's neck.

Give the command, "Rex, HEEL!" and walk forward with the dog. Go 10 to 20 feet and stop, having the dog at your left side. Say, "Rex, SIT" and make him sit next to you. Then pet and praise him. Continue heeling and sitting the dog for about 20 minutes. Make certain to give the command to heel a second before you step forward and give the command to sit as soon as you stop walking.

Talk to him in a praising voice when he is coming along with you and be sure to pet and praise him well each time you get him to sit. Loosen the choke collar when he is sitting and rub his chest and throat with your left hand as you orally praise him. Always make certain that the choke collar rings are again situated at the right of the dog's neck before you begin to heel him.

If the dog is still fighting the leash, lagging, foraging, attempting to get between your legs, or going over to your right side, handle it as described under Heeling Problems in the last chapter.

Heel the dog in the pattern of a square, making square corners when you turn right. If the dog is coming along with you quite well, begin teaching him to make left turns as well as about-turns. Pivot properly on your turns and make square-cornered turns. However, if your dog is still having problems on the heeling, concentrate more on getting him to heel with you and to sit when you stop rather than worry too much about getting square turns.

If the dog is coming along without a struggle, begin walking at a fairly fast pace. After about 20 minutes of heeling and sitting, give him a 10-minute recess. To begin the recess, take the dog off command as was done yesterday, by telling him "Rex, OKAY!" Pet him and remove his leash by unsnapping it from the choke collar. Then walk a few feet out in front of him and face him as you repeat the "Okay" command and also give the hand command by raising your arms up in the air. Do this two or three times, and if he gets the idea and comes to you, pet him real good, saying "Rex, Okay! Good boy!" and let him run around. Feed him a few pieces of meat as you talk to him and pet him. Then let him relax for a few minutes before continuing with the lesson.

Instructions for Sit/Stay Exercise

After a rest of about 10 minutes, attach the leash to the dog's choke collar. Pet him and talk to him for several seconds as you adjust his choke collar and properly take hold of the leash. Again heel and sit the dog two or three times. You are then ready to begin teaching the Stay command.

This exercise consists of giving the Stay hand and oral commands to the dog as he sits at heeling position. Quickly step out in front of the dog and face him from a distance of only 2 or 3 feet. Keep the dog sitting for about a minute while you talk to him in a praising voice. Return to heeling position by walking around the dog from right to left and again stop at the dog's right side. Pet and praise the dog well.

Two different hand commands for the Stay command are used in this exercise: one when standing at the dog's side (at heeling position) and one when standing in front of the dog. The Stay hand command that is given when leaving the dog's side is illustrated in Fig. 3. The Stay hand command that is given at a distance from the dog is shown in Fig. 4. These hand commands are also described on page 28. The Stay hand command is the only hand command that is given at the dog's side. With the exception of the off-leash heeling hand command, all other hand commands are used only when out in front of the dog or away from him.

Several problems are often encountered in teaching a dog this exercise, but he should learn to do it correctly within several days. The first problem

FIG. 3. Stay hand command when given at heeling position beside dog.

is that the dog is going to want to follow you as you step forward to stand in front of him. Be prepared for this and quickly apply a firm, backward jerk with the leash (toward the rear of the dog) the instant he attempts to follow. Sometimes, it will take two or three repeated corrections to convince him to stay as you step forward. Frequently, corrections on this have to be quite firm to get the dog to remain sitting as you move away.

As you prepare to leave the dog, hold the leash in your right hand only for the moment and take one step forward with your right foot as you simultanously say "Rex, STAY!" (using the hand command with your left hand) (Fig. 3). After giving the hand command, grasp hold of the leash with the left hand to be prepared to jerk him back if he attempts to follow you, which he will do the first few times he sees your left foot move forward.

Step out in front of the dog as quickly as you can while he remains sitting. Be sure *not to pull on the leash* as you move away from him. If you do, you will cause him to come forward.

If you have to correct the dog for not staying as you attempt to get away from his side, keep repeating the oral command to stay as you jerk the leash backward.

When you get out in front of the dog, keep the leash slack and hold it in your left hand so you can continue giving him the Stay command with your right hand. Stand 2 or 3 feet in front of the dog, facing him, and say, "Rex,

FIG. 4. Stay hand command when given away from dog.

FIG. 5. When dog breaks from sit position and stands up or attempts to go to trainer, he must be promptly put back into sitting position by applying a jerk on the leash angled toward rear of dog.

STAY . . . STAY . . . STAY . . ." as you repeatedly give the hand command, making a pushing motion with your right hand. If he remains sitting, add a few "good boys" as you repeat the command (Fig. 4).

The first few times you do this exercise, the dog may decide to get up and come toward you. If he does, quickly move close to him and push the leash at an angle toward his rear with little jerks and get him back into sitting position (Fig. 5). This procedure is the same as when working on the Sit command when away from the dog, which will be discussed later. Tell the dog, "Rex, STAY!" as you correct him. As soon as you get him back in sitting position, slacken the leash and move out in front of him again, saying "Good boy . . . Rex, STAY . . . STAY" as you keep giving the Stay hand command with your right hand. Keep the dog sitting for a minute or two, before you return to heel position.

Return to Heel Position (Trainer Procedure)

This is basically a simple accomplishment. However, it should be done in a particular manner until the dog also learns it. To return to heeling position, all you actually have to do is walk around the dog, by walking slightly to your right, circle his rear (stepping over his tail), and walk forward to stand on his right side (heeling position).

The first few days you do this, the dog isn't going to understand what you are trying to do. He may try to come to you or swing around to watch you walk around him. He is supposed to *stay sitting* until you get back to heel position to pet him and complete the exercise. If the dog gets up as you approach to your right of him, quickly correct him with a jerk angled toward his rear to get him sitting again. Then move out in front of him again and keep saying "Rex, STAY . . . STAY . . . STAY!" as you keep making little "pushing" motions with your right hand (Stay hand command). Since he did not stay as you returned to him, you do not want to immediately go to heel position to pet him. He must learn he has to obey the command. Keep him sitting for a few seconds and then attempt to return to him. If he stays sitting, circle him and stop on his right side. Then kneel down next to him and put your left arm around him as you scratch his chest with your right hand and praise him. A dog knows he is *really* being praised when you make body contact with him and pet and talk to him. A little pat on the head means nothing.

When you are returning to the dog, make certain you do not pull on the leash and cause him to break his sit. Keep the leash slack, but do not let it drag on the dog. If you brush against the dog or touch him while circling him, you will cause him to break his stay. If your dog will remain sitting while you circle him on your return to heel position, talk to him in a praising voice as you approach and circle him so he will know he is doing right. Do so each time you make your return to him.

After having the dog do his first Stay exercise and after completing praising him at his side, stand up and give him the Heel command. Heel and sit him four or five times, then repeat the Stay exercise. Continue doing this for about 45 minutes. You can take another 10-minute recess but make sure to take the dog off command when you are ready to do so by using the Okay command.

When you finish the lesson for the day, take the dog off command, pet him, and feed him some meat. Spend at least 10 minutes petting, talking, and/or playing with him after the lesson.

Always make certain to end your last exercise for the day with *praising*. If the dog doesn't do his last exercise accurately and has to be corrected, repeat it until you can end the last exercise for the day without having to give him a correction, only praise. If you can't manage it on the Stay exercise, then do it with the Sit exercise after heeling. But it is always best to make the new exercise the *last one* you do for the day, as the dog will think about it later.

When working the dog on this Stay exercise, remember that the dog is left sitting each time. He must be made to continue sitting until you command him to heel. If he attempts to lay down at any time, jerk him back up into the sitting position. This also applies when you are petting him at his side and if he stands up. However, do not give him a command to sit when he is on the Stay command. His command is only STAY, but jerk the leash to get him sitting again.

The last 45 minutes or so of the lesson should be spent working the dog on the Stay exercise, with heeling and sitting a few times between each Stay exercise.

For the problems you might have on returning to the dog during the Stay exercise, refer to pp. 108-110.

Most of the rest of the exercises will be done with you giving commands as you stand in front of the dog. Any time the dog requires a correction when you are working in front of him, approach close to the front of the dog and apply the correction as you stand *in front of him*. Do not walk around to the dog's side or rear to correct him on commands given while you are standing in front of him.

Lesson 3

Down Exercise, Away from Dog

Before beginning the third lesson, put the training choke collar and six-foot leash on your dog. Talk to him and pet him for a few seconds. Before starting a new exercise, practice the dog on the same exercises as yesterday for approximately 30 minutes.

Previous Exercises

Begin the lesson by heeling the dog and making him sit each time you stop walking. Before you start, make sure the choke collar is adjusted properly (as you should be doing at the start and finish of *each exercise*). The collar should be loosened frequently when working the dog.

By now, your dog should be heeling and sitting quite well. If you are having some problem with him on any particular phase of the exercise, correct him according to what he is doing wrong by referring to the last chapter. If he is coming along with you quite well, which he should be, you can now give him extra slack in the leash (about 1 foot of slack). Heel him in a square or rectangular pattern, making square-cornered turns (pivoting correctly). Also practice him in making complete about-turns to go in the opposite direction, as well as left and right turns. As always, make certain to give him the command to heel each time you start walking forward, as well as any time you have to correct him for lagging behind you.

By this time, your dog should know he is required to sit every time you stop walking. If he does so most of the time, you can discontinue commanding him to sit when you stop. However, any time he does not immediately sit as soon as you stop walking, correct him and give the oral command, "Rex, SIT!" at the same time. The correction is a jerk at a 45-degree angle toward his rear. By now, these corrections should be quite firm because he has had enough practice that he knows he is supposed to sit. If he should lie down, give him a good correction by jerking the leash straight up and telling him "Rex, SIT!"

After you have made the dog heel a few times, do the stay exercise by giving the hand and oral commands "Rex, STAY!" and quickly moving out in front of him. If he attempts to follow as you step away from him, give him a good backward jerk on the leash toward his rear as you repeat the oral command to stay. When you are out in front of him, keep repeating the oral command to stay as you keep giving him the hand command to stay. Rotate the oral command with verbal praise as he remains sitting. If he lies down, move closer and jerk him up into the sitting position and then back away from him. If he stands up, move in and jerk the leash toward his rear to make him sit, repeating the command. Then back away from him. Stand about 3 feet out in front of him, face him, praise him as he remains sitting, and rotate the hand and oral commands to stay "Good boy . . . Rex, STAY! . . . good boy!" The more often the dog sees and hears his commands, the faster he learns them.

If the dog is staying fairly well, stand 3 or 4 feet in front of him. But any time he breaks, move in fast and correct him, making him sit again. If he has to be corrected, back away from him again and keep him sitting for a few seconds longer before you return to him. He should be kept sitting for at least 1 minute while you talk to him in a pleasant tone. Then return to him by circling him and returning to heel position at his right side. Remember to talk to the dog in a praising voice as you circle him and do not pull on the leash or brush against him. Stay about 1 foot away from him as you walk around him and don't let the leash drag on him because these things tend to cause him to break his sit.

Pet and praise the dog well when you get back to his right side. Make sure his choke collar is loosened and the rings are at the right of the dog's neck. Then give him the command to heel. Heel and sit him four or five times, then repeat the Stay exercise. Continue repeating the Heel and Stay exercises for about a half hour. Don't forget to give the heel command *every time* you start walking. Pet and praise him after each sit.

Each time you leave him on the stay, give the *hand and oral* commands to stay as you prepare to leave the dog and give them *repeatedly* when you are in front of him.

After having worked the dog for at least 30 minutes on heeling and staying, give him a recess by taking him off command with "Rex, OKAY!" Remove his leash and walk out in front of him to repeat the Okay command by throwing up your arms as you say the command. If the dog comes to you, pet and praise him. Any time he hesitates to come, go to him, repeating the Okay command, and pet him excitedly so he knows he can run around. Be sure to feed him a few pieces of meat during his recess.

FIG. 6. The Down hand command.

Instructions for Down Command

After the recess, begin the new command for this lesson. Attach the leash to the choke collar and heel the dog a few times.

Start this exercise just like the Stay exercise. With the dog sitting at your left side (heeling position), give the command to stay and step forward to face the dog from a distance of about 3 feet. If the dog breaks his stay, quickly correct him and get him sitting again. Then back away to about 3 feet in front of him.

From this position, begin teaching the Down command. Give *both hand and oral commands* each time. The oral command is "Rex, DOWN!" The hand command is raising your right hand above your head and then quickly lowering it. Your hand should be outstretched toward the dog with the palm down (Fig. 6).

As the dog remains sitting, give him the hand and oral Down commands. He isn't going to know what it means, but repeat it about three times before you correct him, unless he stands up or tries to come toward you. Correct him by putting your foot on the leash, which pulls the dog's head toward the ground. Press the leash down gently with your foot, but get the dog's head down to the ground (Fig. 7). Some dogs will lie down within a couple of seconds after their head is held down. Others will keep their rear up in the

FIG. 7. Teaching the Down exercise away from the trainer by using foot pressure on the leash to place the dog in the Down position.

air and try to pull backward. But keep your foot on the leash and hold the dog's head down until he lies down. It makes no difference how he lies down—whether on his belly or on his side—just as long as he lies down. Keep giving him the hand and oral commands for Down until he lies down.

The instant you have him down, say "Good boy!" and circle around him to go to heel position at the dog's right side. Kneel down next to him and praise him, rubbing his back, side, or belly and talking to him to convince him you are thoroughly pleased with him. But keep him down while you are doing it. If he should try to get up, quickly grab the leash near the snap and jerk him back down as you say "DOWN!" Continue petting and praising him when you get him back down. When teaching the Down command, give a lot of attention to the dog because most dogs dislike this command more than any other when they are first learning it. So until he learns it really well, spend several minutes petting and praising him to encourage him to be more cooperative. When he knows you are going to overwhelm him with praise and petting when he lies down, it doesn't take long before he begins showing some enthusiasm for the command.

When you have completed the praising and petting for the Down command, stand next to the dog (at heeling position) and say, "Rex, SIT!" Pet and praise him again after you get him to sit. Give the dog the Sit command at the end of each Down exercise, after you have praised him well when he was down.

Continue working the dog on all his exercises, Heeling with Automatic Sit, Sit/Stay, and Down. The order in which you do them makes no difference, just as long as you practice him on all three exercises. Since the Down command is a new command, be sure to get him to do it *several* times and also use it as the final exercise for the day. Spend at least a half hour working him on all the exercises and then end the lesson by taking him off command with the Okay command, as previously described.

Lesson 4

Down and Sit Exercise, Away from Dog and at Heel Position

Put the choke collar and six-foot training leash on the dog. Pet him and talk pleasantly to him for a minute or so before beginning the work. Make certain that the choke collar is on correctly and adjust it so the rings are on the right side of the dog's neck.

Previous Exercises

The first 30 minutes of the lesson should be spent practicing the dog on his previous exercises. Begin by heeling the dog, making certain he sits each time you stop walking. Give the command "Rex, HEEL!" each time you begin to walk, going 10 to 20 feet for each heel. As usual, use a square or rectangular pattern, making left and right turns and about-turns as well as walking in a straight line. If the dog is doing quite well, hold the leash in only the right hand while heeling the dog by slipping the loop handle over your right thumb and grasping hold of the leash about 2 feet from the end, giving the dog a fair amount of slack. If he has to be corrected on sits, hold the leash with the left hand also to give the correction.

You should also be trying to get your dog to sit correctly on the automatic sit when you stop walking.

Heel the dog a few times, then do the Stay exercise. Heel him a few more times, then do the Down exercise, and so on, so he gets practice on all three exercises.

Heeling should be done at a fairly fast walking pace now. If you walk too slow, many dogs are inclined to begin lagging.

If you need to refresh your memory on the Sit/Stay or Down exercises, refer to the previous lessons because you must make the dog do them correctly.

After working the dog for at least 30 minutes, take him off command by saying, "Rex, OKAY!" (using hand and oral commands) and remove his leash. Give him a 10-minute rest.

Instructions for Down and Sit Exercise, Away from Dog (Hand and Oral Commands)

The Down and Sit exercise will be separated into two parts. The first part will be done from in front of the dog, using both hand and oral commands. The second part will be the Down and Sit command at heeling position, using the oral command only.

To start the exercise, the dog should be sitting at your left side at heeling position. Give the Stay command orally and with your left hand (just as you have been doing on the Sit/Stay and Down exercises). Walk out in front of the dog and face him from a distance of about 4 feet. Then give him the Down command orally and with your right hand, as before. Repeat the command two or three times if necessary. Then correct him by placing your foot on the leash if he doesn't obey. Always say the command *loudly* when you correct the dog. If you had to correct him, again back away from the dog

FIG. 8. The Sit hand command.

so you are standing about 4 feet in front of him. Orally praise him as he lies down, for about 30 seconds. (Make sure he remains down.)

As you continue standing out in front of him, say "Rex, SIT!" and give the hand command for sit at the same time (Fig. 8). Your hand is motioned *downward* (with the palm facing down) to tell the dog to *lie down*. Your hand is motioned *upward* (with the palm facing up) to tell him to go *up* to sitting position. The dog quickly catches on to this.

Give the hand and oral commands to sit three or four times. The dog probably won't respond because he doesn't know what he should do. His only association with the Sit command has been when heeling. So, after repeating the hand and oral commands a few times, if he hasn't done it, move directly in front of him and jerk him up into sitting position as you say "Rex, SIT!" As soon as you have him in sitting position, reach down and rub the sides of his neck with both hands as you say, "That's a good boy!" Loosen his choke collar at the same time. Then back away from him again about 4 feet and continue to verbally praise him for several seconds as he remains sitting. If the dog should break his sit by standing up, lying down, or attempting to move away, quickly move in and correct him, getting him back in sitting position. When working from in front of the dog, any corrections

FIG. 9. Teaching the Sit exercise away from trainer, by swinging leash upward as the command (hand and oral) is given.

that must be given should be applied from in front of the dog. Fig. 9 shows another technique to make dog sit.

After praising the dog for sitting for a few seconds, return to the dog by circling him and going to heel position at the dog's right side. Then kneel down next to him and put your left arm around him and scratch his chest with your right hand as you tell him what a good boy he is. Keep him sitting while you praise him.

When you finish petting and praising him, stand up; and without another word walk forward again, out in front of the dog. His last command was "SIT" and he must continue to obey it. If he doesn't, correct him and get him sitting again.

Again, from a distance of about 4 feet in front of the dog, give the Down command (hand and oral). Repeat the command a few times and then correct him with your foot on the leash if he doesn't obey. As soon as you have him down, praise him orally from 4 feet away.

Then command him "Rex, SIT!" (making certain to give the hand command with your right hand also). Repeat the command about three times before you correct him, if necessary. If you have to correct him again, do it the same as before. Go right in front of him and jerk him up into sit position, then reach down and scratch the sides of his neck, loosening his choke collar as you tell him he is a good boy. Then back away 4 or 5 feet in front of him and continue orally praising him for several seconds. When you finish praising him, again return to heel position to pet and praise him some more. After praising and petting him at his side, stand up and give him the command to heel a few times.

Instructions for Down and Sit Exercise (at Heel Position on Verbal Commands)

The purpose of this exercise is to give the dog practice on the Sit and Down commands as well as on the verbal commands, which are usually more difficult for the dog to learn.

To do this exercise, start with the dog sitting at heeling position. Give the oral command only, "Rex, DOWN!" If the dog doesn't respond, hold the leash tightly with your right hand and have the slack in the leash a few inches above the ground (the distance from the ground depending on the size of your dog). Put your foot on the leash and press the dog's head to the ground as you repeat "Rex, DOWN!" until he lies down (Fig. 10). As soon as he lies down, say "Good boy!" and bend down and pet, and praise him for a few moments.

After praising the dog, stand erect and say "Rex, SIT!" Pet and praise him as soon as you get him to sit.

FIG. 10. Teaching the Down exercise at heel position with foot pressure on the leash (using oral command).

Have him do the Down and Sit exercises at heeling position two or three times. Then heel him a few times.

Spend the remainder of the lesson on working the dog on the Down and Sit exercises from in front of the dog (with hand and oral commands), the Sit and Down exercises at heel position on verbal commands only, and the Sit/Stay exercise. Between each of the exercises, do the Heel with Automatic Sit. At the end of the lesson, take the dog off command with the Okay command.

Lesson 5

Come (Recall) and Finish Exercise

Begin this lesson by putting the leash and choke collar on your dog and petting and talking to him a little before you begin working him. Don't forget to adjust the choke collar so that the rings are on the right side of the dog's neck, which you should do at the start of every exercise.

Previous Exercises

Begin the lesson by heeling the dog a few times, making certain that he sits each time you stop walking. Then work him on all the exercises in the previous lessons, having him do each of them a few times. Heel him two or three times between the different exercises. Remember, the more practice a dog gets, the faster he learns and the better he becomes at performing the exercises. If there is some exercise your dog is not doing very well, work him more frequently on it until he can do it well. The dog should be doing all these exercises quite well by now, so if you are not getting good results on some exercise, refer to the last chapter. If a dog has to be frequently corrected to get him to do one of these previous exercises, make certain you are doing it correctly. If you are, you may have to correct your dog more firmly. Some dogs require a very firm correction to get them to respond. After working the dog steadily for at least 30 minutes, take him off command with the Okay command. Remove his leash and let him relax for 10 minutes.

Instructions for Come (Recall) and Finish

The Come (Recall) and Finish exercise (at heel position) involves teaching the dog to come, on command, and sit in front of you. When you command him to HEEL, he gets up, walks around you, and sits at your left side. This is called the *Finish*.

To teach this exercise, begin as you do with the Sit/Stay. Two commands (hand and oral) are involved. The oral command for Come is "Rex, COME!" The hand command is pointing your right forefinger at the ground just in front of your toes. Each time you give the hand command, shake your finger in a pointing direction toward the ground to emphasize the hand command, making a one-stroke downward motion with your hand. This hand command can be repeated as often as necessary while teaching the command to the dog. Hand commands must consist of *motion* to be readily observed and learned by a dog. If you were to stand with your right hand down in front of you with your finger pointed at the ground but your hand still, the command would be difficult for the dog to learn or understand. Your hand and finger must be sharply projected in a downward *movement* to enable the dog to understand.

The oral command for the Finish is "Rex, HEEL!" The hand command is given with the right hand held downward, making a "wave" toward your rear (Fig. 11). This hand command is more exaggerated when training a dog than what is normally required after a dog is well trained. During training, this hand movement is about 2 feet in length.

The exercise should be started with the dog sitting on the Stay command while you face the dog from a distance of about 5 feet (as far as the leash will permit and still not be tense). Stand erect on this exercise and don't move

FIG. 11. The Finish at Heel exercise.

from your position. Do not move closer to the dog (unless he has to be corrected for not staying prior to giving the Come command) and do not move farther from the dog once the command is given. Bend only to pet the dog. By this time, your dog should be *staying* on the Stay command, so a correction should not be required.

To start the exercise, first give the dog the Stay command (hand and oral) as he sits at heeling position. Then walk out in front of the dog as far as the leash will permit (and still not put tension on the choke collar). Face the dog, holding the leash with the left hand because the right hand must be used to give the hand command.

Praise the dog for staying, by saying "That's a good boy," then give the command "Rex, COME!" as you sharply point your finger toward your toes. Give the hand and oral commands two or three times (Fig. 12). The dog may or may not get the idea of what you want. If he starts to come toward you, immediately begin praising him orally. If he doesn't understand, apply short, little jerks on the leash (toward you) as you again point your finger toward your toes. Keep shaking your finger at your toes as you say, "Rex, COME! . . . Good boy . . . Rex, COME!" until the dog begins to come toward you. The instant he starts to come, stop jerking on the leash and say

FIG. 12. Trainer gives the Come command (hand and oral) and applies little, short jerks on the leash until the dog begins coming toward him. The command and oral praise are rotated while getting the dog to come.

"Good boy! . . . Rex, COME!" If he only takes a step or two forward and stops, again apply a little jerk on the leash as you repeat the hand and oral commands, saying "Good boy . . . Rex, COME!" until he is directly in front of you. As soon as he is in front of you, reach down and scratch the sides of his neck with both hands (loosening the choke collar) as you tell him what a good boy he is.

If your dog is particularly resistant to obeying your command and repeated jerks on the leash, you may have to gently pull him all the way to you the first few times. Don't be rough with the dog during the first couple of days he is learning this exercise. Many dogs will respond more quickly and willingly if the trainer is gentle. After a couple of days of practicing an exercise, correction must be firmer when a dog doesn't respond to show him that he *must* obey.

When you have gotten the dog in front of you and petted and praised him for coming, the next step is to get him to sit in front of you, facing you. Many dogs will do so while you are rubbing their neck and praising them. If your dog doesn't sit on his own, tell him "Rex, SIT!" Apply an upward and backward jerk on the leash, if necessary, to get him to sit (Fig. 13). Bend down and scratch his neck and praise him some more. After petting him, take your hands off the dog and stand erect as you continue talking to him in a praising voice (as he remains sitting in front of you).

In preparation for teaching the dog to go around you for the Finish to sit

FIG. 13. Dog is placed in sitting position after coming to trainer by applying a mild jerk on the leash at a 45-degree angle toward the rear of the dog.

at heel position, transfer the end of the leash behind your back into your left hand. As soon as you have done this, give the command "Rex, HEEL!" and motion with your right hand, giving the hand command for the Finish. The dog isn't going to understand what you want him to do, so you must repeat the hand and oral commands several times. Then grasp hold of the leash with your right hand and apply repeated short jerks on the leash, toward your right rear, as you continue commanding the dog with "Rex, HEEL!" When you get the dog to your right side, begin applying short jerks on the leash with your *left* hand until you get the dog to walk around your right side, behind your back, and then to heeling position at your left side. When you get him at heeling position, command him to sit and correct him with a backward-angled jerk on the leash, if necessary. Then pet and praise him when he is sitting and loosen his choke collar.

By rotating praise with a command, the dog realizes you want him to do something. He isn't *sure* what he should do, but my instructions of how to *show* him make it easy for him to guess right and your words (praise rotated with the command) give him the encouragement to try it (Figs. 14 to 18). Consequently, the dog learns quickly.

FIG. 14. After giving hand and oral commands to heel, leash is switched to right hand. Trainer takes one step back with right foot.

FIG. 15. Dog is then pulled to trainer's right rear.

FIG. 16. Trainer switches leash, behind him, to his left hand and takes one step forward with his right foot while pulling dog forward to his left side.

FIG. 17. With his right foot, trainer moves dog's rear so dog is in a straight line at trainer's left side.

FIG. 18. While giving the Sit oral command, the trainer jerks the leash at a 45-degree angle toward dog's rear as he pushes the dog's rump down with the instep of his right foot.

It is sometimes difficult to get large dogs to go around you until they begin getting the idea as to what they are supposed to do. Even some small dogs will dig their front feet into the ground and try to pull back, against your little jerks. With these dogs, you may have to jerk a little more firmly and shove their rump around behind you with the heel of your right foot. But after eight or ten times of doing this exercise, most dogs begin to understand what you want them to do.

Repeat the Come (Recall) and Finish exercise several times. Heel the dog a couple of times between each Come and Finish exercise or again give the Stay command after praising the dog for the Finish he just completed and go from there, leaving the dog sitting where he is and walking out in front of him to do the Come and Finish again.

After working the dog on the Come and Finish exercises several times, have him do all the other exercises a few more times each. Then do the Come and Finish a couple of more times, as the final exercise for the day. End the lesson with the Okay command (hand and oral), remove the leash and training choke collar (if you are using a larger size than normally), and pet and praise the dog. Feed him a little meat, as usual, and spend a little time with him to give him some attention and fun.

Lesson 6

Stay While Heeling Exercise (Motion Exercise)

Prepare your dog for the lesson by putting his training choke collar and six-foot leash on him. Adjust his choke collar as usual, making certain that it is loose and that the rings are on the right side of the dog's neck. Pet and talk to him a little before you begin working him.

Previous Exercises

The first half of the lesson should be spent working the dog on his previous exercises. Start the lesson by working the Heel with Automatic Sit exercise a few times. Do this exercise a few times between each of the other exercises. Do the other exercises in any order you want. The best procedure is to have the dog do the exercises about three times each and then repeat the cycle several times. This way the dog gets enough practice on each exercise and yet it doesn't become tiresome for you or the dog by repeating an exercise too many times at once. The more exercises a dog learns, the more time you must spend working him because a dog must do every exercise a number of times each day to improve.

When working the dog on the Finish exercise, give the hand and oral commands once or twice before you jerk the leash to make him heel. This will enable you to know when the dog is catching on to the command and willing to do it, thereby avoiding unnecessary correction. A smart dog will learn the Finish exercise by the second day he is worked on it, but some dogs take longer to learn it because they require more practice to remember an exercise. If you have to jerk the leash to get the dog to go around you, keep repeating the oral and hand commands as you jerk the leash, until he gets to your right side. Continue repeating "Rex, HEEL!" as you continue applying jerks until the dog is in the heel position.

When you are ready for a rest period, take the dog off command with "Rex, OKAY!" using the hand command also. Remove his leash and let him run around or relax for about 10 minutes. Be sure to always give him a little meat to eat while he is off-command.

Instructions for Stay While Heeling Exercise (Motion Exercise)

On this exercise, the dog will be given a command to stay when you are heeling him. After giving the command to stay, toss the leash aside, to your left, and continue walking forward another 10 feet or so (Fig. 19). The dog should stay where he is when commanded to stay. After walking about 10 to 15 feet beyond the dog, stop and turn to face the dog and praise him orally for several seconds (as he stays where he is). Then return to the dog, circle his rear, and stop at heel position to pet him and end the exercise.

This particular exercise, without a doubt, becomes one of the most practical and frequently used of any exercise. It is also the one that is often most urgently needed in numerous, everyday situations. It will keep your dog from running out the door or the gate when you open it or jumping out of the car when you don't want him to. It will also stop a dog that is about to chase

FIG. 19. Teaching the Stay While Heeling exercise. Trainer has tossed the leash aside while giving oral and hand commands to stay. Trainer continues to walk away while dog stays.

something. When your dog becomes proficient in this exercise, you will wonder how you ever survived life with a dog without this training.

To teach the dog this exercise, first do the Heel and Automatic Sit a few times. When you stop, pet him on the chest with your left hand and say "Good boy!" as he sits at heel position.

Then give the Heel command again and walk forward, holding the leash in your right hand. Walk forward about 10 feet and without stopping or pausing, suddenly say "Rex, STAY!" (simultaneously giving the hand command with your left hand). The instant you have given the command, toss the leash aside to your left (in front of the dog) and continue walking forward without slowing your pace.

The dog should stop when you give him this command to stay. *Do not* turn your head to look back at him as you walk forward because that will encourage him to follow you. However, watch him out of the corner of your eye as you continue walking forward another 10 to 15 feet from the dog. The dog must stay, but he may take a step or two forward after you command him to stay because he will be a little unsure the first few times he performs this exercise. Usually the dog will remain standing, but sometimes he will sit or lie down. As long as the dog *stays* that is all that is necessary. However, if the dog continues following you after you command him to stay, quickly turn around and pick up his leash and apply a short, sharp, straight-backward jerk (toward his rear) and emphatically say "Rex, STAY!" Immediately drop the leash again and turn away from him to walk forward. When you are 10 or 15 feet out in front of the dog, stop and turn around to face him and begin praising him orally for several seconds (as he stays). If he decides to come toward you, immediately say "Rex, STAY!" and give him the stay command with your right hand, making a pushing motion as shown in Fig. 4. If the dog continues to come toward you, quickly go to him, grabbing hold of the leash and correcting him with a stout backward jerk as you repeat the command. Then walk away from him to stand 10 to 15 feet out in front of him. *But do not turn your head back to look at him as you walk away.* You must watch the dog out of the corner of your eye to make certain he doesn't try to follow you.

After praising the dog from a distance for several seconds, return to him, praising as you walk. Circle his rear and stop at his right side (heeling position) to pet and praise him with plenty of enthusiasm.

On this exercise, you have to be quick to correct the dog if he keeps following you. Don't wait until you have walked 10 or 15 feet before you notice whether he is following you. If he is still following by the time you have taken three or four steps after commanding him to stay, don't lose any time about giving him a fast correction. Be sure to emphatically repeat the command when you correct him.

After petting and praising the dog at his side, pick up the leash and give him the command to heel. Heel him two or three times and then repeat the Stay While Heeling exercise. Have him do this exercise three or four times and then work a few times on another exercise. Then do this exercise a few times again.

Spend the rest of the lesson practicing the dog on all the exercises. If a dog doesn't do too well on some exercise, you must work him on it more frequently rather than repeat it too many times in a row.

As the final exercise for the day, do the new exercise, stopping when the dog does it correctly and really praise and pet him when you return to him. End the lesson for the day with the Okay command. Pet him and feed him some meat.

Lesson 7

Beginning Distance Training

This lesson consists of drilling the dog on the commands and exercises he has already learned. However, you must begin changing your procedures by starting to work farther away from him in preparation for off-leash work.

The actual lessons now should last at least 1½ to 2 hours as the dog now has quite a few exercises he needs to practice. In addition, you should be starting to work at longer distances from him, which means each exercise will take a little more time as you will have to often go to him to pet him or correct him as well as do some walking around while he is on a command. He must now begin learning not only to remain on a command, but to do so for a longer period. If a dog is particularly nervous and inclined to whine or keep getting up when kept on a command for more than a minute or two, you should keep him down for a longer period, constantly correcting him and putting him back in position if he repeatedly gets up before you give him another command. With this type of dog, you can put them on a Down command just in front of or to your side while you sit in a chair. Keep the dog down until he has remained down (without getting up) for about 5 minutes. Anytime he gets up, repeat the Down command as you correct him, putting him back down. It might take 15 minutes before you convince him to *stay* down for 5 minutes, without getting up. This method produces faster results than having to walk 20 feet to correct him ten dozen times. He will then do much better when you are working away from him. If you only have three working speeds (slow, slower, and stop), you will have to spend more time to give your dog the drilling he needs.

Previously, when working away from the dog, you would go out to the end of the leash. However, to get the dog accustomed to working farther away from you in preparation for the beginning of off-leash work, drop the leash as you walk about 10 feet away from the dog to do these previous exercises.

On the Come (Recall) and Finish exercise, after giving the dog the command to stay, toss the leash to your left so it is out of the dog's way. Then walk out about 10 feet in front of him to give the Come command. Be sure to always praise the dog orally while he is coming to you. If you drop the leash in front of the dog, he will likely step on it when he attempts to come to you (and refuse to come any further). If the dog does step on the leash, go to him and release the leash from under his foot. Then back away and give him the command to come again.

Be sure you are also giving the hand commands on every exercise.

As soon as the dog is doing fairly well at 10-foot distances on the exercises during which you leave his side (Sit/Stay, Down, Come and Finish, Down and Sit on hand and oral commands), begin increasing the distance you go from him about 5 feet at a time. If you suddenly go too far from the dog, he may start breaking and running. He may do so occasionally anyway, but you want to avoid this, if possible. Make sure he is working fairly well at one distance before you increase it, particularly on exercises in which the dog has to do something (such as come, sit, or lie down) while you are at a distance away from him. When beginning distance work as well as during the early stages of off-leash training, the dog will learn more quickly and be more cooperative if correcting is minimized. A dog learns to do something through *doing it.* Too many or too frequent firm corrections can upset a dog and make him run away at every opportunity. This problem can be eliminated or at least minimized by reducing the amount of correcting and/or using a larger percentage of mild corrections when he doesn't obey a command during the first few days of this training. While practicing the dog on the Sit and Down commands, repeat the commands two or three times, if necessary, to encourage the dog to do them without a correction. If the dog still does not obey, begin slowly walking toward him as you again repeat the hand and oral commands loudly. If the dog obeys before you get to him, say "Good boy" and walk on past him, circling him to return to your previous standing position. If the dog does not obey the command by the time you reach him, he does have to be corrected to make him do it. However, make the majority of your corrections moderate in intensity. If your dog has to be *repeatedly* corrected on a command, *then* give him a really firm correction to make an impression on him.

Occasionally, when working on the Stay While Heeling exercise, instead of returning to the dog, give him the command to come (followed by doing the Finish). But make sure you toss the leash out of his way when you give him this command.

The exercises for getting the dog started on working at longer distances are the Stay, Sit, and Down. On these exercises, the dog does nothing but remain on the command until you return to him. You can go 25 or 30 feet away from the dog and leave him on each command for about 2 minutes before you return to pet him. While the dog is remaining on a command at distances, you should talk to him in a praising voice occasionally so he knows you haven't forgotten him.

To do the Stay exercise, merely give the dog the command (hand and oral) to stay as you leave him sitting at heel position. Drop the leash and walk away about 25 feet. Sit down or walk around him in a big circle while he stays. (It is preferable to rotate these actions.)

On the Stay command, it doesn't matter if the dog lies down or stands up, as longs as he *stays*. However, if he stands up, he may be thinking about coming to you or taking off, so quickly give him the hand and oral commands to stay. If he comes toward you or takes off, quickly go and pick up his leash and gently lead him back to where he was and correct him *at that spot* for not staying. Be sure to place him so he is facing his original direction before you correct him. Then give him a sharp and firm backward jerk with the leash and say "Rex, STAY!" Drop the leash and walk away. When the dog has stayed for at least a couple of minutes, return to him, circle his rear, and stop at heeling position to really pet and praise him extra well.

To practice him on the Sit and Down commands, give him a Stay command while you are at heeling position. Walk out in front of the dog about 10 feet and give the hand and oral commands for Down. Praise him orally and walk farther away. If you want to do the Sit exercise, after giving him the command to lie down, follow it with the command to sit and then walk farther away. The command you want to practice him on must be the last command you give him. And, of course, he must be made to obey it before you walk away from him.

The Sit and Down commands are automatic *stays*, and the dog must also remain in that position. If he changes his position, you must correct him for the command you gave him. If he comes to you or takes off, you must go get him and lead him back to where you left him and then correct him at that spot for the command he broke. But make certain you get him facing his original direction before you correct him. Emphatically repeat the broken command as you correct him. Then drop the leash and walk away again. After the dog has remained on his command for a couple of minutes, return to heeling position and really pet and praise him.

As the dog becomes better at performing these exercises, you can make him stay for a longer period if you wish. Five minutes is about the limit for leaving a dog in the sitting position, but you can leave them on a Down command for a longer period. I often leave a dog on the Down command for as long as 10 or 15 minutes after he has had enough practice doing this. But while he is learning, and particularly when he has many exercises he needs to practice, 2 or 3 minutes is sufficient.

On the exercises for today, if the dog comes toward you or runs off when you are working away from him with the leash laying on the ground, you must correct him. If the dog breaks a Stay, Sit, or Down command, you must quickly lead him back to where he was before he broke the command and correct him at that spot for the command he broke.

If the dog runs off after you gave him the Come command, go and get the dog, catching hold of his leash. Instead of taking the dog back to where he was when commanded to come, *take him to the spot he should have been if he had obeyed the command to come.* Upon breaking the command to come, lead the dog back at a run or very fast walk. As you do so, apply three firm, sharp jerks in the direction you are heading. With each jerk, say "Rex, COME!" When you get back to where you had been standing when you gave the Come command, sit the dog in front of you and facing you, just exactly as he would have been if he had obeyed. Then pet him and give the command "Rex, HEEL!" and make him do the Finish. Pet and praise him when he goes to heel position and sits there.

When you take a rest period or end the lesson for the day, be sure to take the dog off command with the Okay command.

Lesson 8

Beginning Off-Leash Work

By now your dog should know all the commands and exercises he has been taught, and he should be ready to take the first steps toward working off leash. For this lesson and for the next few days, attach the shortie leash to his choke collar. Attach the six-foot leash to the choke collar also. There is plenty of room on the choke ring to accommodate the snaps of both leashes. The shortie leash is left on the dog throughout each lesson as this enables you to correct the dog faster and more easily than attempting to grasp hold of the proper ring on the choke collar. However, do not hold on to the shortie leash. It is only for the convenience of giving speedy corrections.

The next few days are going to involve switching the dog to off-leash work. This can be accomplished in a couple of days with a smart dog. However, the majority of dogs are only average in intelligence, and more time and repetition are required to get these dogs trained.

The principle of teaching a dog to work off leash involves repeated attempts to get him to do his commands and exercises off leash. If he has to be corrected, it is done with jerks on the shortie leash. If he responds poorly or not at all, the six-foot leash is put back on him and he is worked on the exercise for a few minutes on leash. Correcting when on the long leash must be very firm. Remove the long leash and try the dog off leash. This is done repeatedly, until the dog learns that he must also work even though he is not on leash.

Most dogs will not work dependently off leash so they have to be gradually taught to do so. Once the dog learns that being off leash is not going to allow him to escape having to work, he much prefers it to leash work because it is much more pleasant and he does not receive all the jerks he gets when the long leash is on him.

This training phase is partly psychological. When the dog is being worked off leash, the corrections are milder compared with on-leash corrections. You must give a lot of terrific praise and petting. The dog must be encouraged to obey by frequently repeating his commands and rotating the commands and oral praise.

However, if a dog will not obey a command off leash or requires repeated correction, the six-foot leash is reattached and he is worked for a few minutes on the exercise he is not doing. Corrections given him with the long leash must be firm when he doesn't obey immediately. When he is given a command, he must do it! Your praise and petting (when his poor response demands he be put back on the long leash) should be shorter and not as excited as when he obeys off leash. You have to show the dog that everything is better if he obeys off leash. If he doesn't obey off leash, put the long leash back on and be very stern if he doesn't obey immediately.

After several days of practicing to get the dog to work off leash and he is still trying to avoid off-leash work, the corrections with the shortie leash must also get stiff to prove to him that he must do it.

If a dog runs off during off-leash work, he must be caught and the six-foot leash put on him. He must also be severely corrected. How he is corrected depends on the situation. The Heeling and Come exercises are handled differently from other commands, so refer to the last chapter.

It is usually not difficult to get a dog to work off leash on the exercises in which he stays in one spot. The ones that require the most repeated drilling are the Heeling and Come exercises. These two exercises are also the ones during which dogs are most likely to run away.

Anytime you remove the long leash to try to get the dog to work on his commands off leash, always remove the long leash when you are praising at heeling position. Do it with as little fuss as possible. You don't want to make "a big thing" out of taking the leash off, so do it with as much discretion as possible. Many dogs will work quite well for a little while, thinking they are still on leash.

By now you should know how to work your dog on leash on all the exercises he has learned. If you forget something or are not sure, always refer back to the original lesson. If you are having a problem on any exercise, consult the last chapter.

To begin the lesson, work the dog on the six-foot leash. Heel him a few times, doing the Automatic Sit each time you stop walking. Pet and praise him after each sit. Then have him do all his other exercises at least once, on the leash: the Sit/Stay, Down (from in front of the dog), Down and Sit at heel position on oral commands, Down and Sit (in front of dog) on hand and oral commands, Come and Finish, and Stay While Heeling (dropping the leash).

Do not repeat commands during on-leash exercises. The dog should know them well by now, and if he doesn't obey he deserves a firm correction. If the dog does not do well on any particular exercise, have him do it about three times. If you have to correct the dog at any time, repeat the command as you correct him, using a harsh tone of voice.

Heeling Exercise

To begin heeling off leash, first heel the dog a few times on leash. On your last Automatic Sit, reach down and unsnap the six-foot leash from his choke collar and roll it up in your hand. Say "Rex, HEEL!" and give the hand command as you step forward. The hand command you use can be your choice of snapping your fingers or holding your left arm down at your side and making a forward wave with your hand—the *reverse* of the Finish hand command.

If the dog heels with you as you walk forward, promptly praise him by saying "Good boy!" and continue walking a few paces. Then stop and make the dog sit by jerking backward on the shortie leash, if he doesn't sit automatically. Continue doing the Heel with Automatic Sit several times. Pet him enthusiastically after each sit.

If the dog doesn't immediately come with you as you step forward, step backward and repeat the heel command as you apply a sharp jerk forward on the shortie leash and take a step forward again. Be sure to praise him as soon as he comes along with you.

If the dog stops at any time while you are heeling, quickly stop and turn the upper part of your body toward him and say, "Rex, HEEL! . . . Good boy . . . Rex, HEEL!" as you keep repeating the hand command. If he still won't come forward to your left side, move straight back to heeling position, and with your left hand, apply a sharp jerk forward on the short leash and firmly repeat the command and step forward again. If the dog then comes along at heel, praise him orally as you walk.

You have to keep an eye on your dog when heeling him off leash to make sure he is coming along with you. If he stops, make sure you also stop before you get more than two or three steps away from him. Then try to encourage him forward by saying "Rex, HEEL! . . . Good boy . . . Rex, HEEL!" as you keep repeating the hand command. If he won't respond, retrace your steps to heeling position, give him a correction with the shortie leash, repeat the command, and step forward again. You may have to do this repeatedly to get him to heel off leash. If you have to repeatedly correct him to get him to heel, jerk harder on the shortie leash when you correct him.

Work the dog in this manner for 10 or 15 minutes. If you have to repeatedly keep correcting him to get him to heel with you, put the long leash on him again and heel him with that a few times. If he lags at all, does not immediately start heeling when you step forward, or does not sit promptly when you stop, give him a firm correction with the long leash.

If the dog does not sit, correct him with a jerk toward his rear. If he lags or does not heel immediately, give him a good, sharp jerk forward with the long leash. Repeat the command harshly when you correct him. You do not ordinarily tell him to sit on the Automatic Sit, but if he has to be corrected for not sitting, tell him "Rex, SIT!" when you correct him.

After working him on leash for a few minutes, when you are standing at heeling position, remove the long leash again and roll it up in your right hand. Try him on heeling off leash again.

You will have to follow this procedure every time you work him on the off leash heeling until he will do it well. You should work him on off-leash heeling two or three different times each day. The sloppier he is, the more practice he needs. Be sure to do a lot of praising when the dog is heeling off leash. When you have to use the long leash to get him to heel, reduce the praising while you are working him on leash. Pet him and say "Good boy" after each sit, but say nothing else except to give the command to heel.

Don't swing your arms back and forth as you walk when heeling the dog or the dog will think he is getting a Stay command and will stop heeling with you.

Sit, Stay, and Down Exercises

Work the dog for awhile on each of these exercises, walking out a distance of at least 10 or 15 feet each time you leave him. If the dog is doing quite well, you can even walk a little farther away. As you keep him on each command for a couple of minutes, occasionally go and sit down to watch him. Other times, walk around him in a big circle. If he breaks his command or changes position, move in and correct him, repeating the command. Then quickly walk away again. After he has remained on a command for a couple of minutes, return to him by circling his rear and pet and praise him well at heeling position.

If you aren't having much trouble with the dog running off on these exercises, you can take off the long leash. Otherwise, leave the leash laying on the ground, attached to the dog, to make it easier to catch him and correct him. Be sure to correct him properly if he runs off by leading him back to the spot he had been and then giving him a firm correction at that spot for the command he broke.

Have the dog do the Down and Sit exercises at a distance on both hand and oral commands. The dog should know these commands well enough now that you should practice him sometimes on only hand commands and sometimes on only oral commands. Do the same with the Stay command.

If your dog isn't responding well on these three commands, put the six-foot leash back on and work him for awhile on the Stay, Sit, and Down commands at a close distance with the leash, just as when he was learning these commands. If he doesn't obey every command immediately, correct him emphatically. Heel the dog a few times on the leash between these exercises.

Stay While Heeling Exercise

If the dog will heel off leash, work him on this exercise off leash. If not, use the long leash to heel him a couple of times and then give him the hand and oral commands to stay while you are walking. Make sure the dog stays when you command him to do so. Walk out a distance of 15 or 20 feet from the dog and face him. Praise him orally as he stays for a couple of minutes. If he leaves the spot, go get him and lead him back to where you left him and turn him to face his original direction. Then apply a stout backward jerk on the leash as you say, "Rex, STAY!" Drop the leash and walk away again. Walk around the dog in a big circle. Stop at heel position and pet him.

Heel him several times again and then repeat the Stay exercise. Occasionally give the Come command when you are standing in front of the dog, instead of returning to him every time. Then have him do the Finish exercise. Practice the dog on this exercise several times but heel him a few times between each Stay command. To avoid working the dog in a routine, change the order in which you practice the exercises.

If you are working the Stay While Heeling with the long leash, when you give the Come command and the dog comes and sits in front of you, pick up the leash as you pet him and then give him the hand and oral command to heel (Finish) at your left side.

Come and Finish Exercise

Begin teaching the dog this exercise off leash by heeling him a couple of times on leash. As you stand at heel position, remove the long leash. Then give the hand and oral commands for Stay and walk out in front of the dog. Start by going about 10 feet away from the dog. As he becomes better at performing the exercise, gradually increase the distance until you are about 30 feet from him. As you face the dog, tell him he is a good boy and then give the command "Rex, COME!" as you shake your right forefinger to point toward your toes. Repeat the command two or three times, if needed, to get the dog to come to you. Praise him orally as he comes.

If he will not come, walk up in front of him and apply a sharp jerk forward on the shortie leash as you say "Rex, COME!" Quickly back away from him a few steps and say "Rex, COME! . . . Good boy!" When he gets in front of you, get him to sit there (if he doesn't do so) and pet and praise him for a few moments. Then give him the hand and oral command to Finish at heel position. Pet and praise him well when he does so.

There are usually only two problems encountered with the Come command, off-leash—either the dog may not want to come to you or he may run off. For the proper way of correcting him for running off on the Come command, refer to the preceding lesson and to the last chapter.

Difficulties with the Finish exercise (at heel position) after doing the Come exercise are a little more varied but not difficult to correct. Some dogs will attempt to do the Finish exercise before you give them the command because they know that is the next thing they are going to be required to do. Some will try to go directly around you without stopping to sit in front of you, and others will sit behind you. Still others will not sit when they get to your left side, but they will try to go around you again or sit in front of you. The solution to these problems can be found in the last chapter under Finish On Leash and Off Leash.

Spend at least 1½ to 2 hours working the dog repeatedly on all exercises. When you take a rest period or after completing the lesson for the day, be sure to take the dog off command with the "Okay" command (and hand command). Pet him, play with him, and feed him some meat.

Lesson 9

Stand Exercise

Begin the lesson today by attaching both the six-foot leash and the shortie leash to the same ring on the choke collar. If you have been using an extra-long choke collar, you should now use the normal size for your dog as most of the work from now on should be off leash. This normal size choke collar can be left on the dog at all times. If the dog is a puppy, check the collar frequently to make sure that it isn't too small as the dog grows.

Always start out working your dog by using the long leash on him and beginning with doing some heeling with automatic sits. This calms the dog down so he realizes it's time for work. Correct him for anything he doesn't do properly. After each sit, pet him on the chest and rub his throat with your left hand as you say "That's a good boy!"

Begin practicing him on all the commands and exercises he has learned. When you start working him on performing off leash, remove the six-foot leash when you are standing next to him at heeling position and petting him so he doesn't notice the removal.

Spend as much time as possible repeatedly trying to get him to perform well off leash, as described in the previous lesson. There should be consider-able improvement in the performance of your dog each day, and by now he should be quite good at performing his exercises. If he isn't or has to be corrected often, you very possibly are not correcting him firmly enough. A dog has very thick skin and hair and strong neck muscles, and he can take much more of a correction than most people think.

In my private training, I normally have a dog fully trained by the ninth day and all that remains is to practice the dog and train the owner. The dog is usually quite steady off leash by this time. I tell the owner that it is now time for him to begin working his own dog, just as I have been doing each day while the owner watched. Almost invariably, when the owner begins work-ing his dog, the dog will not perform well. When the owner gives the dog a Down command, for example, the dog may lie down and then sit back up or stand up and look at the owner as though he had no idea as to what he was supposed to do. When the dog will not do a command, I instruct the owner to correct the dog. After repeated correction and repeated disobedience by the dog, I have to constantly keep reminding the owner that he is not correcting the dog firmly enough to get the dog to work for him. People tend to back-off if their dog lets out a faint whimper when they correct it, thinking they corrected him too hard. When a dog knows a command and won't do it, it is simply because he is not being corrected properly or firmly enough to convince him he should and must do it.

The dog's response to commands will tell you when you have corrected him hard enough. When he will obey your commands, you know you have gotten through to him and he is willing to recognize you as master. But at the same time, don't forget to give a lot of praise and petting when he obeys. This is another mistake people tend to make repeatedly. They will pat their dog and then ignore him. You have to *talk* to the dog to let him know he is doing what you want him to do.

Today you will start teaching the dog a new command. You should spend about 15 minutes working on it and then go to the other exercises for a while. Then do the new command again for about 5 minutes and then do something else again. Your dog needs repeated practice every day on each command and exercise he has learned. You also have to get him used to working at gradually greater distances from you. By the time your dog is finished, he should easily obey commands from 75 to 100 feet away. However, until your dog requires few corrections, a distance of 20 to 30 feet is more desirable because you do have to keep returning to the dog every time you have to correct him. The more often you have to correct him, the more often you have to go and pet him. *Praise and correction have to balance the scales.*

Instructions for Stand Exercise

This exercise consists of teaching the dog to go from a Down or a Sit position to a Stand position on command. The dog will learn to do this command at a distance, and you should not have to touch him to make him stand up once he learns it.

The oral command is "Rex, STAND!" The hand command is given with the right hand, which is held flat, palm facing up, and moved from your right to left just in front of your waist in a "slicing" motion as though you were slicing the air in front of your body. One motion, from right to left constitutes giving the command one time (Fig. 20).

To teach the dog this exercise, put the six-foot leash on the dog. When the dog is sitting at heeling position, give the Stay command and walk out in front of the dog about 1 foot and slightly to your right of the dog. Facing the dog, give the hand and oral commands three or four times.

Holding the leash in your left hand, put your right foot under the dog's belly and lift up, forcing him up on his feet as you apply repeated short jerks

FIG. 20. The Stand hand command.

FIG. 21. Teaching the Stand exercise by using the foot to lift the dog into a standing position while applying little jerks on the leash in a forward and upward direction.

on the leash toward the front of the dog, in a slightly upward direction (**Fig. 21**). As you keep making short jerks with the leash and holding the dog up with your foot, keep saying "Rex, STAND . . . Rex, STAND . . . Rex, STAND!"

The instant you feel that the dog is taking some of his weight off your foot, remove your foot from under his belly and say "Good boy!" and stop jerking on the leash. Be sure to slacken the leash instantly. The dog will probably try to sit immediately. Quickly put your foot under his belly again and lift upward as you again jerk on the leash and say the command over and over. The very second you feel he is putting his weight on his own feet again, stop jerking the leash and remove your foot and again say "Good boy!"

Keep repeating this procedure until you are able to get the dog to stand, even for a few seconds—long enough to praise him and gently stroke his back (but don't put any pressure on his back or he will sit again) or rub the side of his body with the fingertips of your right hand. Verbally praise him as long as he stays standing. If he sits down, repeat the hand and oral commands and quickly put your foot under him again to lift him up as you begin applying short jerks with the leash and saying "Rex, STAND . . . Rex, STAND."

Remember to slacken the leash and remove your foot the instant he stands and gently stroke and praise him. As soon as he will remain standing long enough for you to stroke him and praise him for a few seconds, drop the leash on the ground and quickly move away from him. Walk around him in a small circle, staying 5 to 6 feet away from him. Orally praise him as you walk around him. If he tries to sit down again, quickly move in front of him and pick up the leash. Give him the hand and oral commands again. If he doesn't stand up, begin jerking on the leash again as you lift him up with your foot, continually repeating the command.

Keep repeating this procedure until you are able to get the dog to remain standing for about a minute as you circle him. Then go to his side at heeling position and pet and praise him, but don't let him sit down while you are doing it. If he sits down, quickly make him stand again.

As soon as you have managed to keep the dog standing long enough to circle him and pet him at heeling position, pick up the leash and give him the command to heel. Heel him once or twice and then repeat the Stand exercise by giving the dog the command to Stay and going in front of the dog to give the Stand command.

After doing this a few times, if the dog doesn't stand on command, apply an upward jerk (to the front of the dog) as you repeat the hand and oral commands to see if he will stand. If not, lift him up with your foot as you apply rapid jerks on the leash and keep repeating the command.

Work the dog in this manner for 15 or 20 minutes. At the end of that time, the dog will very likely go to the standing position on command. Be sure to praise him and stroke his side each time you get him standing, before you walk away.

Work the dog on this exercise again during the lesson and for a few minutes at the end of the lesson. As soon as you can get him to stand on command or at least by applying a jerk on the leash in an upward direction to the front of the dog as you give him the command, end the lesson after you pet and praise him for standing.

As soon as the dog does the Stand exercise without you having to get him up with your foot, begin giving the command from 3 or 4 feet out in front of him.

When he begins doing it on command (without having to jerk the leash), progress to giving him the command to stand from a distance of 8 or 10 feet using the shortie leash instead of the six-foot leash. As the dog continues to improve on the command, give the command from greater distances.

After a couple days of practicing this command, if the dog doesn't obey the command, apply a firmer forward and upward jerk on the leash as you repeat the command. If he still doesn't stand, go to him and get him up with your foot and a stout jerk on the leash as you harshly say the command.

While the dog is learning this command, walk around him in a circle while you keep him standing. This will teach him to stay where he is. When he begins to know the command quite well, which he should after three or four days, stand in one spot if you wish. However, if he begins coming to you then give him the Stay command. If he doesn't obey the command to stay, go to him and give a sharp, backward jerk on the leash as you say "Rex, STAY!" Then walk away. If he sits down after you have to correct him for not staying, quickly go to him and lift him with your foot and give him a good Stand correction by jerking the leash away from the front of the dog in an upward direction. When you correct him, say "Rex, STAND!" and walk away the instant you have him standing. Then orally praise him from a distance for about a minute before you return to heeling position to pet him.

Using your foot and jerking the leash to get the dog standing does not have to be done on any certain side of the dog. If he sits when you are at heeling position or when you have walked around to his right side, you can also get him standing again from his side that is nearest to you. The leash must always be jerked in an upward direction, toward the front of the dog, however. If you are standing in front of the dog, giving him the command to stand, the leash must be jerked *toward you* but in an *upward* direction.

As the dog gets better at doing the stand exercise you should be able to walk up to either side of him and stroke his neck and back while he remains in standing position. Walk away and then return to pet him. He should easily be able to learn to remain standing for several minutes at a time.

When you are ready for a rest break and at the end of the lesson, remember to take the dog off command.

Lesson 10

Teaching the Dog to Come When Not On Command and Starting Distraction Work

Today's lesson consists of giving your dog some good drilling practice on what he has learned. It is also time to begin adding some new twists to his lessons, which will broaden his training and teach him more stringent obedience to your commands to develop your control over him.

Previously, lessons were always begun by heeling the dog on the six-foot leash. It is time for him to learn that he must obey your commands, no matter what he is doing when he is given a command and no matter what is happening around him.

At this point, corrections must really be severe (except when working the dog on the Stand command, which is still new). A dog has to learn by degrees, one step at a time. Your dog should have had enough practice by now on all his exercises to be performing them well. If your dog still runs off when he is off leash, you must correct him severely each time he does it.

Teaching the Dog to Come When Not On Command

To get ready for the lesson, put the choke collar, but not the leash, on your dog. Let him run around the yard or do whatever he is doing. Walk out into the yard and give him the command to come ("Rex, COME") using the hand and oral commands. Repeat the command no more than three times. If he comes to you, orally praise him and get him to sit in front of you. Then pet him as you talk to him in a praising voice, pause and then give the Heel command for him to Finish at heel position. Really pet and praise him after he does it.

However, if the dog would not obey your command to come, go to him and attach the six-foot leash to his choke collar and correct him with three firm jerks forward as you emphatically repeat "Rex, COME!" with each jerk.

Rush back with him to the spot you stood when you commanded him to come to you. As usual, make him sit in front of you, facing you. Then pet him by rubbing the sides of his neck as you praise him and command him to heel. Make him go to heel position if he doesn't do so immediately; pet and praise him after he does.

If your dog obeyed your command to come, start working him on his various exercises. Put the shortie leash on him and begin working on off-leash heeling with automatic sits and practice all the other exercises as well. Make him do his exercises off leash, but if he starts making mistakes, put the long leash on him to work him for a few minutes so you can correct him harder. Then try him off leash again.

If your dog did not obey your Come command, after you have corrected him for not coming and made him do the Finish, pet him and say "Rex, OKAY!" and let him run around for a couple of minutes. When he isn't paying any attention to you, give him the Come command again. If he obeys the Come command this time, pet him when you have him sitting in front of you. Make him do the Finish, pet him again, and go on to the other exercises. However, *repeat* the procedure of giving him the Okay command followed by the Come command in a couple of minutes until he *will* obey the command to come to you. Each time he doesn't obey it, correct him severely. *He must obey the command to come* before you do anything else.

Work your dog for about a half hour on the various exercises. When working on the Stand command, use the long leash since this command is still new to the dog.

Take the dog off command for a short break, and when you are ready to work him again, try giving him the command to come again, when he isn't paying attention to you. Walk out into the yard to do it, but wait until he is lying down or doing something where he isn't paying much attention to you. If he doesn't obey the command to come, put the long leash on him again and correct him with it as before. Make him sit in front of you, pet him, make him do the Finish at heel position, and pet him again. If he obeys the Come command, continue with the lesson. If he doesn't, keep giving him the Okay command after he does the Finish and follow it with the Come command again in a few minutes, until he will come to you on command.

Work the dog on this every day at the start of the lesson, during rest breaks, and at the end of the lesson by giving him the Okay command and then waiting for a few minutes before commanding him to come. But after today, give him the command to come only once—loud and clear. If he doesn't obey it, get him and correct him soundly with the long leash.

At mealtime, when your dog is eating, walk out 20 or 30 feet from him and give him the command to come. When he comes, pet and praise him well, give him the Okay command (without doing the Finish), and let him finish his dinner. But if he doesn't come on command, you must go and correct him with the leash. If your dog has to be repeatedly corrected for not coming, you either aren't doing it properly or aren't making your corrections strong enough. Be sure to pet and praise your dog each time after you get him to come and sit in front of you and again after having him finish at heel position.

Starting Distraction Work

The purpose of working a dog with distractions is to develop control over the dog under all conditions. Most training procedures use distraction work, but do not put it to its best use; consequently, poor control is actually developed over the dog under most conditions. A distraction can be anything that takes the dog's mind and attention away from you, causing him to ignore or break your commands.

When training a dog, distractions are a hindrance to the training. But once the dog learns his commands, distractions are a necessity to teach the dog he must obey your command regardless of anything else. Few trained dogs will obey commands from their owner when something exciting is happening around them because they were not properly trained with distraction work. Several types of distractions can be used for training a dog, and several different methods can be employed to make use of them. However, not every distraction has the ability to grasp and hold the attention and interest of every dog. The distractions that provide the best control over the dog and are shortcuts for this type of training are those distractions that particularly appeal to the individual dog. You can make use of many different types of distractions when training your dog, but it is very important to include a couple that particularly appeal to your dog.

Dogs are easily intimidated with the use of distractions that are not all that interesting to them. Distraction work consists of working your dog on his commands and having a distraction nearby. The dog will ignore your commands or break a command he is on to concentrate on the distraction. This is where firm correction comes into play. Eventually, the dog will ignore everything but what you are telling him to do if you make good use of distractions and correct him *firmly enough* for any disobedience.

But most trainers use distractions that are not of any great interest to the dog. So after getting one or two small corrections, the dog is no longer interested in the distraction and will obey his commands. But let a tremendous distraction come along and your dog is gone! However, if you *train* him with those kinds of distractions and give him some really firm corrections for any disobedience, he won't forget what happened the last time he didn't obey your command when one of those great distractions came along.

Distraction training outside a fence should be started on leash. You can also work your dog with many distractions inside a fence, and this will give you added control, in preparation for working the dog off leash around a really fascinating distraction. You must first develop control over your dog before you attempt working him off leash around something he really enjoys doing, such as chasing a cat. If a distraction is difficult to use inside a fence, place it just on the other side of the fence, but still close to the dog. Close distractions are always more interesting to a dog than distant ones.

Every dog has its own particular forms of interest. For example, a dog that seldom goes out of his own yard might be very interested in the activity of other people and dogs in the local park, whereas a dog that is accustomed to going for walks is not going to think anything of such distractions. Such things would provide a very poor distraction for him. You have to look for things that really interest your dog. If you don't know what does, experiment with different types of distractions. Some dogs get very excited about someone riding a bicycle. Other dogs love chasing cats. Meat is a good distraction for practically every dog. Sometimes a strange dog is exciting for a dog. If you use a strange dog for a distraction, be sure to do so with a fence between the two dogs or with both on leash so you don't end up with a dog fight instead of a training session. Determine what types of things are good distractions for your dog and then use them.

To begin working a dog with distractions, put the six-foot leash on him so he cannot run off to chase the distraction. You must also be close enough to correct the dog soundly and quickly. If you work him loose, inside a fence, the distraction must be close to the other side of the fence and you must be near enough to the dog to correct him firmly and immediately. Inside a fence, you can use the shortie leash on the dog to correct him if you wish. You must give extremely firm corrections for disobedience, and you must correct *immediately,* so you must be near enough to the dog to do it.

When working a dog loose, inside a fence, if you have an especially good distraction that makes your dog get carried away to the extent that firm leash corrections will not bring him under control, there are other corrections that can be used. One is a *foot correction.* It is a very effective correction for every dog and is especially good for large dogs since they often require a harder correction than what many dog owners are able to give. Using the top of your foot (the instep, *not* the toe of your shoe) kick the dog under his chest, directly behind the front legs. This correction knocks the wind out of the dog. Do *not* use the toe of your shoe since a hard kick with the toe can injure a rib because it cannot be properly used and directed to make an impact against the bottom of the chest. Correctly done, this kick does not injure the dog. It is no different than a person receiving a slap on the chest from another person's open hand. It must be done directly behind the front legs, however, and not in the stomach area. This correction will bring practically any dog under control, no matter how carried away he might be. But the correction must be properly applied and with sufficient impact for the size of the dog. It is also an effective correction for breaking up dog fights, and you don't have to get your hands in the way where they are liable to get bitten.

Another good correction is a *skin twist*, but this correction must be applied quickly because some dogs are likely to try to bite if you are too slow in completing this correction. It is applied by quickly grabbing a handful of skin on the dog's neck, giving a fast twist, jerk, and then letting go.

After giving one of these corrections, sternly repeat the command, and your dog is almost certain to obey. Most dogs can be handled by giving them a really stiff leash correction for the command they disobey. But if you can't control your dog with a leash correction, use one of these firmer corrections.

Instructions for Distraction Work

The general procedure is to work your dog on leash on his commands: Heeling with Automatic Sit, Sits and Downs (with you in front of the dog, but holding the leash), Come and Finish, and Sit/Stay. Don't use the Stand command with distractions yet because this command is too new to the dog. The older commands are ones your dog should know well, and he should be firmly corrected for not obeying immediately or for breaking a command.

On distraction work, the dog must obey each command immediately. There is likely to be a lot of stalling by the dog because he will be paying attention to the distraction rather than to what you are saying. No stalling should be permitted. When a command is given, the dog must obey it immediately or take a firm correction. For example, if the dog is on a Down command and breaks it by getting up, he should be immediately corrected by emphatically stamping the leash to the ground with your foot. Corrections must be the proper leash correction for the particular command given, but give them firmly. The Heeling exercise and Sits and Downs (away from dog and at heel position) make good commands for distraction work. You are able to give good, stout corrections on these commands.

Cats make a terrific distraction for many dogs. However, it is difficult to use a grown cat as a distraction because it will usually take off the first time the dog lunges at it. A kitten, about 6 to 10 months old, usually works best.

FIG. 22. Teaching the dog to perform on leash in the presence of a distraction.

But don't have anyone hold the cat in case it gets frightened and scratches the person. Having an assistant toss bits of meat on the ground for the kitten will usually keep it occupied while you work the dog on his commands. No danger to the cat should be permitted. Our purpose is to train the dog, not see how many cats your dog can exterminate in the process.

In the presence of the cat, begin working your dog, on leash, on his exercises, heeling him around, back and forth past the cat (Fig. 22). But stay at a distance of about 10 feet from the cat so your dog cannot lunge and grab the cat before you are able to correct him. You must be prepared for your dog to break and be quick to correct him emphatically. If he attempts to lunge at the cat when you are heeling, quickly turn in another direction, applying as firm a jerk on the leash as you can, and say "Rex, HEEL!" and continue walking. When the dog is no longer lunging at the cat, begin working him on Sits and Downs at a distance where he cannot grab the cat before you can act. If he doesn't immediately obey each command, correct him immediately and severely. Usually, after just a few corrections (if they are firm enough), the dog will not pay any attention to the cat. In fact, he won't want to even look at the cat. If he does keep looking, you haven't completely changed his mind yet. Your dog is either very determined or you haven't corrected him firmly enough to convince him to forget the cat.

However, unless your dog breaks a command or doesn't immediately obey a command, you can't correct him. So the next step is to start working him on Sits and Downs a little closer to the cat. If he then disobeys or tries to break away, give him a good correction. If he still obeys but keeps one eye on the cat, you will have to resort to trickery. Put the dog on a Down (or Sit) command, stand 3 or 4 feet away from him, and being talking to someone (or yourself) as you look around and pretend you forgot all about your dog and the cat. *But watch him out of the corner of your eye!* Keep the dog there for 2 or 3 minutes as you appear to be someplace else mentally. Don't talk to your dog! Let him let his mind wander—to the cat. If he lunges or breaks the command he is on, quickly get to him and correct him strongly.

When you can work your dog on his various commands, back and forth and around the cat, without the dog missing a single command, it's time to end the cat distraction for the day. You have convinced your dog (for today at least) that the cat isn't worth the correction.

Food is probably one of the easiest distractions with which to work, but you must be very quick or the dog will have the bait before you know it.

Meat is the best type of food to use. To make it interesting to the dog, he has to know what it is. Start the exercise by having the dog sitting at heel position (on leash). Hold the meat in your partially closed hand and pass your hand near his nose so he can get a sniff of it, but don't give it to him. Instead, toss it on the lawn a few inches to his left and about 3 feet out in front of him. Stand where you are for a few moments to see if the dog will attempt to get the meat. If he does, give him a firm Sit correction.

Then make him do the Down and Sit a few times, but make sure the meat is not close enough to him that he can reach it when he is lying down. It must be just far enough out of his reach that he would have to get up or crawl closer to grab it. If he does, give him a good correction for the command he is supposed to be on and sternly repeat the command. If the dog promptly does each command, pet and praise him.

If the dog decides to do his commands without making an effort to get the meat, heel him away from the spot and return in a few moments, putting him on a Down command so his nose is no more than a foot from the meat. Keep the leash slack and stand there for a few moments. Each time he makes a move to take the meat, correct him quickly and firmly. Try putting him on a Sit command and talk to someone for a few moments or turn your back toward him, as though your attention were elsewhere. If he then attempts to take the meat, correct him soundly.

When the dog quits attempting to steal the meat, work him on other commands—back and forth past the meat, away from it, and back near it—to see if he will make any attempt to disobey a command or break a command to try to get the meat. Make sure he knows where the meat is even if someone calls his attention to it by picking it up and dropping it again near the dog, but just out of his reach. Each time your dog obeys his commands without attempting to take the meat, pet and praise him. Each time he tries to get the meat, stalls on doing a command, or breaks a command to try to get the meat, correct him firmly.

If the dog is on a Down command and tries to crawl closer to the meat, give him a good slap across the nose with the end of the leash. If he is on a Sit command and tries to move to get the meat, give him a good Sit correction. If he is on a Down command and gets up, apply a firm Down correction by pressing the leash to the ground with your foot.

If the dog should manage to grab the meat before you can correct him, firmly hit him across the nose with the end of the leash and immediately force the meat out of his mouth by placing your left hand over his muzzle, grasping his upper jaw, and squeezing his lips against his teeth. This pinches his lips, and he will automatically open his mouth. Let the meat drop on the ground and do not permit him to pick it up.

When the dog does not make any further attempts to get the meat, discontinue the procedure for the day. Pet and praise him, give him the Okay command to release him, and *give him the meat*.

When working a dog with distractions, you must not do any scolding or yelling at the dog. In fact, don't do any talking to him except to give commands and pet and praise him when he does well. You may talk to an assistant or someone nearby, but you want to let your dog's mind wander as much as possible on this work to give you the opportunity to teach him self-control and obedience to your commands. Some dogs will not disobey after they get a few corrections if they think your mind is on them or that you are watching them. Work your dog every day for a few minutes on some type of a good distraction.

Spend the rest of your training session on working your dog on all his exercises and be sure to practice him on the Stand command. Each time you stop working the dog, take him off command with the Okay command, pet him, and give him a treat.

Lesson 11

Down (Drop) on Recall (Motion Exercise)

Previous Exercises (Off Leash)

Most of today's lesson should be spent drilling your dog repeatedly on all his previous exercises. Work on getting him to do them well off leash as well as at various distances. Continue using the shortie leash on him to facilitate any correcting you might need to do. If there is any exercise your dog doesn't do very well, he needs more frequent drilling on it until he does it correctly.

When you leave him on a command, you should also be walking around him in a big circle as well as walking away from him various distances. You should be having him do the Down and Sit, Stand, and Come exercises while you are at various distances from him. This will teach him to obey when you are farther away from him as well as when you are next to him.

Be certain to work him with some sort of distraction for a little while each day. You can even turn part of his rest period into a practice session by sitting in a chair while you feed him his meat and make him sit in front of you. Using a small portion of raw ground beef, give him only a small, marble-sized piece at a time as you keep him sitting in front of you on the Sit command. Give him one piece at a time, pausing for a few moments between giving each piece. If he starts acting up by jumping on you, standing up, or trying to grab at the meat, he must be corrected. If he stands up, give him a Sit correction and repeat the Sit command. Don't give him another piece of meat until he has remained sitting patiently for a few moments. If he jumps up on you or tries to grab at the meat in your hand, hit him on the nose and shout "NO!" Then correct him to make him sit again. Keep him sitting the entire time it takes you to feed him all the meat. This is not only good training for him, but it also teaches him self-control.

Instructions for Down (Drop) on Recall (Motion Exercise)

This is the first of three motion exercises you will teach the dog. They will all be done on the Come (Recall) command. This exercise teaches the dog to take the Down command while he is in the process of coming to you. It is an off-leash exercise, and by this time your dog should be doing *at least* reasonably well off leash.

The general format for this exercise is for you to give the dog a command to stay while the dog is sitting next to you, at heel position. Walk out a distance in front of the dog and stand facing the dog. The dog is commanded to come. When the dog has come approximately half way, he is commanded to lie down. The dog is left down for several seconds and then commanded to come (the remainder of the way to you). Upon coming to you, the dog sits in front of you, waiting for the Heel command. When the command to heel is given, the dog walks around your legs to sit at heel position, ending the exercise.

To start the exercise, heel the dog forward (off leash). When you stop, pet him after he sits at your side. Give him the Stay command and walk out in front of him about 25 or 30 feet. Face him and praise him orally, saying "Good boy" as he remains sitting on the Stay command. Then give him the Come command (hand and oral). When he has come one third to half the way to you, quickly say "Rex, DOWN!" using the hand command at the same time.

The first few times, the dog is going to be somewhat startled and unsure. He may stop or he may continue coming toward you, usually slowly and hesitantly. If he stops, but does not lie down or continues coming toward you, take a couple of steps toward him and loudly repeat the command as you raise one foot several inches above the ground and then stamp the ground (to remind him of the Down correction) (Fig. 23). Usually, the dog will quickly lie down. If he lies down, say "Good boy" and go to him to scratch his neck or side and praise him orally for a few moments. Then walk away, going a distance of 10 or 15 feet in front of him.

However, if the dog would not lie down, you will have to go to him and jerk him down with the shortie leash and say "Rex, DOWN!" as you correct him. When he lies down, say "Good boy" (but don't pet him) and walk around him, making a circle to go out in front of him a distance of 10 or 15 feet.

As you again face the dog from a distance, orally praise him for a moment and then say "Rex, SIT!" (using the hand command also). Verbally praise him when he sits or go to him and correct him to make him sit if he doesn't do so.

FIG. 23. Teaching the Down (Drop) on Recall exercise. The trainer stamps his foot to encourage the dog to respond to the Down command.

With the dog sitting facing you, give the Come command ("Rex, COME!"). When he comes to you, get him to sit in front of you. Pet and praise him and then give the Heel command for him to go around you for the Finish and sit at your side. Pet and praise him after he does.

Again, give him the Stay command and walk out in front of him about 25 feet and repeat the exercise.

After doing the Drop on Recall twice, give the command to stay and walk out again about 25 feet and give the Come command. This time, let the dog come all the way to you and do the Finish.

If you give the dog the Down command too many times in a row, he will begin hesitating on the Come command because he will start expecting you to give him the Down command. He has to learn that he is not going to get the Down command every time. You want him to come quickly when you command him to come to you, which he will not do if he begins expecting to get another command while he is coming. If your dog begins coming slowly or hesitating while you are teaching these exercises, have him come all the way to you two or three times in a row before you give him another Down command when he is coming. Praise him when he is coming.

This is one exercise that should not be worked exactly the same way all the time, and there are many variations you can do. Sometimes, when the dog is coming, only have him do the Down and follow that with the Come and Finish. Sometimes give the Come command and when he is coming, give the Down command. Then go to the dog and stand next to him at heeling position and tell him "Rex, SIT!" Then pet and praise him and walk away to give him the Come and Finish. Other times have him do the Down and the Sit and return to heeling position to pet him and heel him a short distance. When you stop, give him the Stay command, walk away, and do the exercise again. Sometimes you can have him do the Down, then the Sit, and then the Stand before giving him the Come (and Finish).

During the remainder of this training, you are going to teach the dog three commands on the Recall—the Down, Sit, and Stay. It is important that these exercises not be worked exactly the same way too often or the dog will start anticipating (performing a command you haven't given him). For example, if a dog is taught to lie down while coming to you and then commanded to come (the way it is usually taught), he quickly learns that after he does the Down his next command is going to be Come and he will start coming on his own. Also, if any one command is given to him while he is coming (Down, Sit, or Stay) and after doing that one command his next command is always *come,* he soon gets the idea that he only has to do one thing and then it's time for him to come to you. He will start coming to you without waiting for your command to do so or in spite of another command that you may give, which he will ignore. Even if you have him do two or three different commands before you tell him to come, if you give them in the same order every time, he soon realizes what the last thing is he has to do before the Come command will be given and he will still anticipate on the Come.

It takes practice on exercises for a dog to be good at doing them, but you do not want him to get used to doing anything in one set routine. You must often fool your dog by not letting him figure out any set pattern to the commands and exercises you are going to have him do. He will then be more stable on his commands and will do exactly what you tell him to do, when you tell him to do it. So never make it a habit to have him do commands in the same order.

Be sure to give him plenty of petting and praising. Always make your dog obey every command given him, correcting him if he doesn't obey, making him do it.

Have your dog do the Down on Recall eight or ten times during the course of this lesson, but don't work him on it too many times in a row. Also have him do it at the end of the lesson.

Be certain to take your dog off command with the Okay command when you begin a recess or finish the lesson for the day.

Lesson 12

Sit on Recall
(Motion Exercise)

Previous Exercises (Off Leash)

Most of the hour and a half or so that you spend working with your dog should be devoted to sharpening him up on his exercises, getting him to perform them correctly and do them immediately, without you having to give him the command more than once each time. Anytime he doesn't obey, he should be quickly and firmly corrected and made to do what he was commanded. The shortie leash will still be kept on him to correct him whenever necessary. You no longer have to do a lot of talking to your dog, except to give commands and to praise him. You should also be practicing distant work as well as close work. Occasionally, work him only on hand commands, then only on verbal commands. Any exercise your dog is not doing extremely well demands more practice than those he does well, but every exercise must be practiced.

Instructions for Sit on Recall (Motion Exercise)

The lesson for today consists of teaching your dog the Sit on Recall, the second of three motion exercises. It is similar to the Down on Recall. The command to sit is given when the dog is in the process of coming to you on the Come command. This is also a simple exercise to teach, since the dog already knows this command. It is just a matter of teaching him to do it while he is moving.

Begin the exercise by giving the Stay command while the dog is sitting next to you at heeling position. Walk out in front of the dog to a distance of about 25 to 30 feet. Turn so you are facing the dog and praise him orally for a moment. Then say "Rex, COME!" and when the dog has come one third to half the distance to you give the hand and oral command "Rex, SIT!" in a loud and stern tone of voice (Fig. 24). If he doesn't sit, immediately begin walking toward him as you repeat the hand command and firmly say "Rex, SIT!"

FIG. 24. Dog given a Sit command on the Recall.

If the dog sits as you approach him to correct him, say "Good boy," and continue walking right past him (without touching him). Walk around him in a big circle, staying about 10 feet away from him. Then go to heel position by coming forward from his rear to stand next to his right side to pet and praise him for a few moments. After praising the dog, walk out in front of him (without saying another word) about 10 or 15 feet, turn and face him, and continue the exercise.

If the dog obeyed the command to sit, immediately begin praising him and go to him, circle his rear and stop at heeling position to pet and praise him. After petting him, walk out in front of him to finish the exercise.

If the dog did not obey the Sit command and you had to go to him and correct him to make him sit, promptly walk back out in front of him about 10 to 15 feet after correcting him. As you stand in front of him, praise him orally for a few moments as he remains sitting.

If the dog should break his sit before you give the next command, quickly repeat the Sit command. If he doesn't obey it immediately, go to him and give him a good Sit correction. When he is again in a sitting position, immediately walk back out in front of him. He must sit on command, and if he doesn't or breaks his sit, he must be firmly corrected and made to sit.

When teaching a dog to do the motion exercises on the Come (Recall), the dog may frequently get quite close to you before he does the command if he doesn't do it immediately or waits until you begin walking toward him. In this event, you should move farther away from the dog so you can give the Come command at a farther distance than where the dog ended up sitting.

After you have made the dog do the Sit on Recall, give him the hand and oral commands "Rex, COME!" When he comes to you, make sure he sits in front of you. Then pet and praise him and do the Finish. Have him do this exercise a couple of times and then have him come all the way to you, without stopping, the next time.

As with the Down on Recall, change the order of the commands to prevent anticipation by the dog. Give him a Down command after he sits followed by a Stand or even another Sit command before you tell him to come. Sometimes just have him come. You want him to learn to do whatever command you give him so don't give them in the same order every time.

The first few times he does this exercise, you should go and pet him after he sits. Then walk away to give him another command. As soon as he begins doing the exercise fairly well, you can stop going to pet him every time he does the Sit command.

As the dog becomes proficient at these exercises, you can begin giving the first Come command from a greater distance, even 75 to 100 feet. But wait until he is working well enough that you don't often have to go and correct him before you increase the distance.

Get your dog to do the Sit on Recall several times during today's training session, but don't work it too many times in a row. Switch to some other exercise for a while. As always, make certain to give the Okay command to release your dog for recess or the end of the lesson.

Lesson 13

Stay on Recall (Motion Exercise)

In addition to teaching the final exercise—the Stay on Recall—continued practice on previous exercises are again on the agenda for today. The new exercise, along with the Down and Sit on Recall, can be practiced at the same time.

Start the lesson by calling the dog to you with the Come command. When he comes and sits in front of you, pet him and give the Heel command for him to do the Finish. Then begin working him on all the exercises.

Every dog should be working well off leash by now. Each dog is different, and they all have their days when they don't want to work, especially during their training period. Some days you may have to do a lot of hard correcting and less praising and petting to convince the dog that he must work and he must obey. Usually, the following day the dog will be a model student.

It should no longer be necessary for commands to be given three or four times before the dog obeys. He should obey each command immediately. If he doesn't, he deserves a firm correction—one that will prove to him in no uncertain terms that you are not asking him to obey you, you are *demanding* it. If a dog finds that he can manipulate you to serve his own purposes, he is going to do it. If he finds he can get out of doing something, he is going to succeed in training *you* rather than you training *him*.

You can also quit giving him meat during rest periods. It's perfectly all right to give him something after his lesson is over, and you should always give him some meat after using meat as a distraction. However, it is time to stop treating him frequently when he works or he will expect it forever.

In addition, it is no longer necessary to pet your dog after every command he performs. This does not mean to quit petting your dog entirely, but instead of petting him after every single command, pet him after every exercise instead. For example, when heeling the dog, you should heel and stop four or five times in a row. So instead of petting him after each sit, pet him when you finish heeling. When you have him do Sits and Downs three or four times each in a row, go and pet him when you finish that exercise. Continue to orally praise your dog when he obeys a command, but you can begin decreasing the amount of praising done each time. Heavy praise is no longer as necessary as when the dog is first learning an exercise; however, always pet and praise your dog for obeying the Come command.

Continue having your dog do every exercise several times during each lesson but switch from one exercise to another, doing each only a few times in a row.

Instructions for Stay on Recall

This exercise is very similar to the Down and Sit on Recall exercises. The dog is given a Stay command while he is coming to you on the Come command. After stopping and staying for a few moments, he may then be commanded to come the rest of the way or he can be given one or more other commands first, such as Down, Sit, or Stand. When the final Come command is given, the dog should come and sit in front of you to await the command for him to finish at heel position.

There is practically no work to teaching this exercise since the dog has already been working on similar exercises and should know the Stay command thoroughly by now through his repeated practice on the stay at heel position and the Stay While Heeling exercise. But just as with anything else, it still requires practice for him to do it on command and do it well and dependably.

Start the exercise the same way you do the Come and Finish exercise and the Down and Sit on Recall exercises by giving the dog a command to stay while he sits next to you at heeling position. Then walk out in front of the dog to a distance of about 25 to 30 feet and face your dog.

Praise him for staying by saying "Good boy." Pause and say "Rex, COME!" (using the hand command also). When the dog is between one third and half the distance to you, say "Rex, STAY!" Simultaneously give the Stay hand command (Fig. 25).

The dog should stop in his tracks and remain standing. If he does, say "Good boy." Pause for a moment and then give him the Come command. When he comes, he must sit in front of you. Pet and praise him and pause a moment before saying "Rex, HEEL!" and also giving the hand command for him to go around you and sit at heeling position, ending the exercise.

If the dog should sit or lie down after he stopped on your command to stay, go to him and give him the Stand correction, getting him back up on his feet. However, do not say anything to the dog as you do this. He should

FIG. 25. While coming, the dog is commanded to stay.

learn that it is automatic for him to Stay in standing position on this exercise. If you say anything to him or give him any command as you correct him to make him stand up, he will start waiting for that command before he will stand. If you had to go and correct the dog to get him standing, walk away ten or fifteen feet before you give him the next command.

On any of these exercises (Down, Sit, or Stay on Recall), the dog must be taught to obey the command as soon as you give it. If he continues coming closer to you after you have given him one of these commands, you must immediately walk toward him and correct him if he didn't obey the command. Correct him by taking hold of his choke collar or shortie leash and leading him back to the spot where he was when you gave him the command. Turn him to face in the original direction and correct him sharply for the command that was last given. On the Stay command, apply a straight backward jerk on his shortie leash and say "Rex, STAY!" Then walk away again to a distance of at least 10 feet from him to give the next command. Dogs always try to get as close to you as they can, so you must correct them for doing so or they will continue to do it. The dog always remembers what your last command was, and he also knows where he was when you gave it to him; that is why you must always lead him back to the original spot. It impresses on him that *that* is the spot where he was to have performed that command.

The Stay on Recall exercise should also be varied from time to time. Sometimes give him the Sit or Down Command, or both, before you give him the Come command to come the rest of the way to you. Other times you can walk up to him, stand directly in front of him, and command him to sit. Then pet him and make him do the Finish. You can use many variations with these exercises and still give your dog the practice he needs on the particular exercise while broadening his training and abilities by not following the same routine all the time. Otherwise, your dog will only do things exactly the way you taught him and he will not obey you when you make any sort of change in his routine. The purpose of training a dog is to secure his obedience. But to make his training more useful and to secure full control over him, you must train him in such a manner that he will learn to obey any command you give whenever you give it. He will then obey these commands whenever unforeseen conditions or circumstances arise.

Always give your dog the Okay command when you are ready to take a recess or quit working him. Pet him and play with him a little after you release him.

Lesson 14

Off-Leash Distraction Work

All the exercises for this training course have already been given. All your dog needs is practice so he will be as perfect as you would like him to be. Today's training session should be spent working the dog on all the exercises you have been teaching him. Since by now you should know how to do all of them, I am going to devote this last lesson to telling you how to make use of off-leash distraction work. This should be done while you are working your dog on his commands and exercises, so you will need someone to help you.

In Lesson 10, I described on-leash distraction work with meat and a cat. You could (and should) be using other types of distractions as well. While you won't need any assistance with the meat distraction, other types (including work with a cat) usually require some outside assistance.

If your dog is well-trained in the previous work, he should have no difficulty whatsoever with this work. However, if you have not already convinced him that you are his master, you will have to put a little more time and effort (and correcting) into teaching him to obey your command off leash in the presence of a distraction.

When working with the cat, it is a good idea to have the long leash attached to the dog's choke collar but laying on the ground as you give him commands from about 10 feet away. This will make it easier to catch and correct him if he should make any move toward the cat. When the dog shows absolute obedience in the presence of the cat, you can begin working him off leash near the cat without risking any danger to the cat.

With the cat kept occupied with bits of meat tossed by an assistant, begin by heeling the dog on leash past the cat at various distances. Begin passing the cat at a distance of about 15 feet. Heel and sit the dog repeatedly, gradually getting closer to the cat, provided the dog does not make any attempts to lunge at the cat. If he does, correct him by giving him a firm jerk the instant he lunges and then correct him for the command he should have been doing when he lunged (Fig. 26).

When you are certain your dog will not attempt to lunge at the cat, drop the leash on the ground and walk out several feet from your dog to have him

FIG. 26. Teaching the dog to perform off leash in the presence of a distraction.

do various commands (Sits and Downs, Come, etc.). Pet and praise him for each exercise he does properly. If he begins stalling on doing a command because he is watching the cat, correct him quickly and firmly for the command he didn't do. If he should run after the cat, catch him quickly and give him a "neck-stretching" jerk with the leash. Take him back to where he should have remained and emphatically correct him for the command he broke.

If your dog makes any attempt to lunge at the cat while you are working him on leash or while his leash is laying on the ground as you stand several feet away, he is not steady and cannot be depended on to obey you off leash or at any distance. There are two reasons for this. Either you have not practiced your dog properly and/or you have not corrected him severely enough for disobedience on distraction work. A dog's response on distraction work, if you are using a good distraction, tells you how much control you have over your dog. If he obeys your every command, you have control over him. If he doesn't, you have not accomplished the desired results and that means you have not corrected him hard enough. Some dogs require much harder correction than others to obtain the same results.

If your dog is steady on his commands with the leash laying on the ground, you can go a little farther out from him, 10 or 15 feet, to give him commands to see if he will continue to obey when you are farther away. If he should decide to break, quickly go get him and correct him. If he still remains steady, you can even get the cat positioned between you and the dog as you give commands. If he continues to obey every command immediately and makes no effort to go after the cat, you know your dog is under control, on leash or off leash.

Off-Leash Meat Distraction

This can be done in the house, on your porch or patio, or in the yard at any time you wish. Give your dog the Down command and sit in a chair 2 or 3 feet away from him. While he is lying down, drop a few balls of raw, ground beef on the floor a foot or two apart and about a foot from his head. As you drop the meat, say "Rex, NO!" in a very stern tone of voice. If he starts to get up, breaking his Down command, firmly correct him by jerking him back down immediately with the shortie leash. If he reaches out to take the meat, quickly grasp his upper jaw with your hand and squeeze his tongue against his teeth, pinching his tongue as you say, "Rex, NO!" He may let out a holler over that and get up. If he does, correct him for the Down.

After about 10 minutes of keeping him down and not allowing him to touch the meat, point your finger near one ball of meat and tell him "Rex, Okay!" and let him have the meat. More than likely, after he eats one ball, he will attempt to take another one. If he makes any move whatsoever to do so, shout "NO!" If he obeys and does not reach for the meat (or if he picked it up and dropped it again), give him the Down command again and make him lie down where he was. However, if he did not obey your No command and reached for the meat anyway, or ate it, quickly correct him again by grasping his jaw and firmly pinching his tongue against his teeth. If the dog ate the second piece of meat after you corrected him for taking it and gave him the Down command, drop another piece near him and say "Rex, NO!" as you drop it. Watch him as he lies there and make sure that he doesn't try to take the meat without getting a good correction for disobeying either your No or Down command. After 10 or 15 minutes, give him an Okay and let him have the meat, ending the exercise for the day. This lesson will also enable you to teach your dog that he must not steal food off the table.

By the end of 14 days, you should have your dog working well off leash on all exercises. That is, of course, provided you have followed instructions for teaching each exercise (consulting the last chapter for any difficulties with your particular dog) and worked your dog sufficiently each day.

Although the training period is over, you shouldn't quit working your dog altogether. A dog still needs practice at least two or three times a week for about an hour each time. He will probably enjoy these sessions because they should consist mostly of praise and petting since little correcting should be required after a dog has learned the commands and exercises. The practice sessions are easy for both you and the dog because the hardest part of the job is over. The dog does most of the work now, but he needs this practice to keep him sharp on his exercises. Practice makes perfect, and it imbeds the commands and exercises so deeply in the dog's mind that they soon become second nature to him.

If you never practice your dog, before long he will become reluctant to do his commands and exercises and will perform very sloppily. He may even begin to forget them. Some dogs don't have good memory retention and can forget almost as fast as they learned. So if you expect him to remember what you have taught him, you must also keep giving him practice on the commands. Your dog's habit of obeying your commands should now be well established, but you must maintain this habit by never giving him a command you don't intend to enforce, should he decide to test your consistency by not obeying a command.

If you have done the work well with your dog, you will continually reap the benefits of owning a well-trained dog. And best of all, the training should have required only about 24 hours of your time!

Training Problems

Heeling Problems (On Leash)
Trainer Pivots Incorrectly

In competition obedience, the dog loses points for body contact with his handler, which usually occurs on turns because the handler does not pivot correctly. You must always pivot on the leg *opposite* the direction you are going to turn. For example, if you are going to turn to your right, pivot on your *left* foot as soon as that foot hits the ground.

It is as much the handler's duty to stay out of the dog's way as it is the dog's duty to stay out of his handler's way when heeling. If the handler does not pivot on the proper foot when turning, his body automatically moves over and bumps into the dog.

Dog Fights the Leash

If a dog is fighting the leash, trying to get loose or away from you, or refusing to come along with you when heeling, give him the command to heel and walk forward. Pull or drag him along, if necessary, but only walk a short distance (6 to 10 feet) at a time. Try to refrain from jerking on the leash until he understands what is expected of him. Keep repeating the command as you walk. The instant the dog begins walking alongside you, say "Good boy!" and walk a few feet further. Then stop, give the command to sit, and make him sit. Then quickly pet and praise him with enthusiasm for 15 or 20 seconds. If the dog is especially nervous about the exercise, spend more time praising and petting him to help him calm down. Most dogs will settle down and begin trying to cooperate with you after 15 or 20 minutes. Occasionally, a dog will not calm down and be very persistent about trying to get loose. Such a dog may require a little more firmness. When they get to the end of the leash in their attempt to get away, apply one or two short, sharp jerks and continue repeating the command as you walk. Sometimes, these dogs will then start jumping on you. If this happens, hit the dog on the nose with the end of the leash. When you get the dog back down, quickly get him to sit and begin praising him. The more correction a dog requires to get him to cooperate, the more you have to compensate with more praising and petting for a longer time.

Dog Bites the Leash

Some dogs will bite the leash when first learning to heel. It is simply a display of frustration on the dog's part. He knows the leash is the cause of pressure on his neck and he doesn't like it. But he will quickly realize this pressure is the result of his own behavior and will stop biting the leash as soon as he finds it no longer hurts when he walks at your side. However, the dog will also bite the leash if you are applying hard jerks on it. Therefore, ease up on your corrections and spend more time and enthusiasm on praising the dog when he sits. Corrections on the heeling exercise should usually be occasional, *short* jerks when the dog lags behind, just sharp enough to get the dog to heel. The command should always be repeated when it is necessary to apply a correction.

Dog Stays Behind

If a dog attempts to stay behind you while heeling, you must repeat the command emphatically and apply very short, sharp jerks forward with the leash. If the dog then speeds up and walks alongside you, praise him orally as you walk. If he still refuses, keep repeating the little, short jerk and command until he does stay at your side. Be sure to orally praise him as you walk when he *does* it properly.

Dog Pulls Ahead

If the dog attempts to drag you or pull as far ahead of you as his leash will permit, he must be corrected. Keep the leash as short as possible while heeling but not so short as to put tension on his neck when he is at your side. When he attempts to go ahead of you, rapidly swing the loose end of the leash in a clockwise circle with your right hand, just in front of your body as you walk. When the dog attempts to pull ahead of you, the end of the leash will slap him under the chin and make him back off from trying to get ahead of you. When you correct the dog this way, make sure to swing the leash in a *clockwise* direction so it slaps him *under* the chin. Swinging it the opposite way would very likely slap him in the face or even hit him in the eye. Slapping him under the chin makes him automatically raise his head and step back.

Dog Attempts to Get Between the Trainer's Legs

This is a common problem with a new pupil and can make you fall down. The dog will always attempt this from behind. There are two remedies. First, try squeezing the dog's head between your legs. If a few times of doing this doesn't cure him, slap his nose with the loose end of the leash. Occasionally, some dogs will dash away to your rear after getting a slap on the nose. If this occurs, make a fast about-turn to your *left*. This maneuver will again get you on the right side of the dog. Take a couple fast steps forward and pull the dog to your left side. Make him sit and immediately pet him.

Dog Attempts to Walk on the Trainer's Right Side

Almost every untrained dog will do this, not only when learning to heel, but whenever he is walked on the leash. Many dogs will go from one side of the trainer to the other. The dog must be taught to remain on your left side. The leash should be held quite short until the dog learns to stay on your left side. When he attempts to get on your right side, for the first several times, make a fast pivot with your left foot, turning to your right, and go in the opposite direction. Give a fast jerk on the leash as you turn around, getting the dog back on your left side. If that doesn't teach him to stay at your left side, slap him on the end of his nose with the loose end of the leash each time he tries to walk on your right side.

Dog Crowds Trainer

Some dogs will frequently press up against your left leg as you walk with them. There are two methods of breaking a dog of doing this. I generally use the first method for the first day or two. If the dog is still doing it after that, I use the second method.

When the dog is heeling and leaning against your leg, start giving him short jerks with the leash, jerking outward *away* from you with your left hand. Repeat these little jerks every time he begins crowding against you. If he continues crowding after a couple of days, begin making fast, sharp, left turns when he crowds. As you turn left (pivoting on your *right* foot) bump him in the shoulder with your left knee. If the dog is small, bump him with your leg or the side of your foot. Each time he crowds you, make another quick left turn.

Dog Jumps on Trainer

When teaching the Heeling with Automatic Sit exercise, some dogs will get excited and try to jump on you when you are trying to get them to walk at heel or as soon as you stop walking (or both). This is a common problem with dogs that have already developed the habit of jumping on people. They want to be petted, and this is their way of trying to force you to pet them. Most dogs can be broken of this habit rather quickly but some others are more determined about it.

If the dog jumps on you from in front, give him your knee firmly in the chest and sharply jerk down on the leash. If he jumps on your back or side, hit him with your left elbow and apply a sharp downward jerk with the leash. If the dog jumps up in front of you or on your side, you can also use the end of the leash to slap him on the nose. Use whichever method is the most effective for your dog. As soon as you get the dog down, correct him for the command he should be doing: jerk forward with the leash if you were heeling; jerk at a 45-degree angle toward the dog's rear if he was supposed to sit. Repeat the appropriate command as you correct the dog.

If a dog has been repeatedly and firmly corrected for jumping on you but continues to do so, have him do the Sit/Stay exercise (Lesson 2). Heel the dog only 4 or 5 feet at a time and then quickly say "Rex, STAY!" At the same time, apply a *stout,* backward jerk on the leash. Then quickly get in front of the dog. Praise him orally only as you keep him where he is for a few moments. Then walk around him to heel position to pet him. As you reach down to pet him, loosen the choke collar and *be prepared* for him to try to jump on you the instant you touch him. If he tries to jump, quickly take hold of the leash near his neck, give him a firm, downward jerk, and then make him sit. Give him the command to heel and walk forward again about 4 or 5 feet. Stop and quickly give him the Stay command and correction at the same time. Move in front of him quickly and continue as above. Work the dog repeatedly in this way until he doesn't jump on you anymore. You can then begin working the Heeling with Automatic Sit and the Sit/Stay exercises according to instructions.

Automatic Sit Problems

Dog Doesn't Sit

When working the dog on the Heeling exercise, some dogs may not want to sit. If repeated jerks at a 45-degree angle toward his rear will not get the dog to sit, use your foot along with the leash correction. Generally, all that is necessary is to put your right foot around behind you and tap the dog on top of the rump with your toe and at the same time, or instantly after, apply the jerks with the leash. If the dog still doesn't respond, tap him harder with your toe or the instep of your foot as you correct him with the leash. Always give the command to sit each time you correct. Praise the dog the instant he obeys.

Dog Sits to Rear of Trainer

If the dog tends to sit behind you when you stop during heeling, give him a short, fast jerk forward with the leash and take three or four fast steps forward. Pull the dog alongside you as you stop. Get him to sit and then pet him. Do this about three times. If the dog still doesn't sit where you want him to, repeat this maneuver, but do it *slowly.* Pull the dog, instead of applying a jerk, and walk slowly, pulling the dog parallel with your body when you stop. This *shows* him where you want him to sit. When you get him to sit, scratch his chest with the fingers of your left hand and praise him orally. Where the dog sits on the heeling exercise becomes a habit with him. If you make a habit of getting him to sit correctly, he will usually do it.

Dog Sits Ahead of Trainer

If the dog tends to sit ahead of you when you stop walking during the Heeling exercise, give him a jerk at a 45-degree angle toward his rear (Sit correction) just as you prepare to stop walking. This will get him to sit next to you rather than ahead of you.

Dog Sits at an Angle in Front of Trainer's Leg

Many dogs will begin doing this if they are petted with the right hand during the praising while sitting at heel position. They want to get as close to the hand that pets them as possible (and still not be too far out-of-line where they might get corrected). If your dog does this, take another step forward, shoving him over with your left leg as you do so. Then make him sit.

The proper way to pet a dog sitting at heel position is to use *both* hands to scratch his neck (and loosen the choke collar) and then continue petting or scratching him on the chest with the left hand only. Or do it only with the left hand. When you pet him with only your left hand, hold your hand straight down at your side. This is where his chest *should* be, and if he gets used to being petted this way, he will also get used to sitting in that spot to be right in line for that hand to pet him.

Dog Sits Too Far Away

The dog should sit approximately 6 inches away from your left leg. If the dog sits fairly close to this distance, do not worry about it until he has had quite a bit of practice at heeling. However, some dogs will sit as much as 2 feet away from you. When this occurs, the dog should be jerked closer and then given a Sit correction, making him sit closer to you. Temporarily petting these dogs on their left shoulder will also encourage them to sit closer. When they start sitting closer, petting on their shoulder should be stopped as it could begin getting the dog sitting too close. Normally, only pet or scratch their chest or throat with your left hand.

Dog Sits Crooked

This is another common problem, especially after dogs are doing off-leash work. *Sitting crooked* means that the dog generally sits with his rear pointed away (outward) from you. When a dog begins doing this, tap his left thigh with the heel of your left foot, making him move closer. If repeated correction with your heel doesn't break him of doing this, reach down with your left hand and grab a handful of hair or skin on his left thigh and jerk his rear closer. This reminder will break even the worst offender of this habit. After a few of these corrections, a forgetful dog will quickly move his rear closer the instant he sees your hand coming toward him.

Dog Lies Down

Some dogs will lie down when they should be sitting at heel position. Correct this habit by promptly jerking straight upward on the leash. At the same time, he should be commanded "Rex, SIT!" If he repeatedly does this, his corrections should be firmer until he stops.

Dog Stands on Trainer's Foot

Some dogs invariably put their right front foot on top of your foot when they are sitting at heel position. To correct the dog, use the toe of your other foot and step lightly on *his* foot, not hard enough to injure his foot, but enough to pinch it slightly.

Return to Dog Problems

Purpose and Procedure

When training a dog to obey commands and perform exercises at various distances away from you, you must frequently return to the dog to pet and praise him as well as complete, continue, or begin an exercise. To accomplish this, you must also teach him to remain where he is and in the position he is while you perform this maneuver. To teach the dog to remain in position, the return to the dog is performed in a particular manner. While no command is given to the dog, it is actually an exercise he must learn to perform, and the dog will learn from *doing*. It usually only takes a couple of lessons for a dog to learn this procedure.

The dog learns this exercise during the on-leash training. Begin by standing a few feet in front of and facing the dog. Each time you return to the dog, approach slightly to your right of the dog, passing on the dog's left, circle the rear of the dog (counterclockwise), and then walk forward, stopping on the dog's *right* side. You will have then made a three-quarter circle around the dog to arrive beside the dog, at heeling position.

To perform this maneuver properly, talk pleasantly to the dog as you approach and circle him, to allay the dog's worries about this maneuver. You *must not* make body contact with the dog until after you arrive at heeling position to pet him. As you circle the dog, maintain a distance of one to two feet from the dog. Normally, the leash is held slack as this is done. However, the leash should not be permitted to drag on the dog, so hold it up slightly when circling the dog. Touching a dog while he is learning this exercise will distract him and cause him to break his position.

While teaching a dog this exercise, you are likely to encounter one of three different reactions:

1. A dog may remain sitting and merely turn his head to watch you walk around him.
2. The dog may get up and attempt to go to you or reach out to touch you.
3. The dog may remain sitting but pivot around in a circle as you walk around him.

Correctly, the dog must remain right where he is and not move until you get to heeling position to pet him. These problems seldom occur when the dog is lying down but occur quite frequently when the dog is in sitting position.

Dog Attempts to Go to Trainer or Touch Trainer

As you approach at a diagonal toward the dog's left side to begin circling him, the most common problem is for the dog to stand up and attempt to go to you or touch you, in an attempt to be petted. If the dog gets up, breaking his sit as you approach, correct him immediately by grabbing the leash a foot or two from the dog's neck and applying jerks angled toward the dog's rear, putting him back in sitting position. As you correct him, repeat *the command last given* to the dog. If it was Stay, say "Rex, STAY!" and if it was a sit command, say "Rex, SIT" (See Fig. 5.) Make certain to use the proper command.

After correcting the dog to get him sitting again, back away from him and praise him orally for a few seconds. Do not return to the dog immediately after correcting him because you want him to learn he must obey his command. After you have kept him sitting for a few seconds, again attempt to make your return to him. If he remains sitting this time, complete your return to heel position and really pet and praise him.

If a dog remains sitting but tries to stretch out toward you, leans into you as you approach his left side, or attempts to touch you, apply pressure to his leash to break him of this habit. Grasp the leash with the left hand a couple of feet from the dog's neck as you approach in front of him and apply slight pressure directly above the dog's head in an upward direction but slightly angled toward the dog's rear. This will hold him in sitting position until you pass his head and get to this left side. Then press the leash outward (away from your body) as you walk past his side. As you step over his tail to pass behind him, slacken the leash and walk forward to heeling position. Then pet and praise the dog thoroughly. Putting pressure on the leash in this manner will quickly teach the dog that he must not try to touch you as you circle him.

Dog Turns Around as Trainer Returns to Heel Position

Occasionally a dog will remain sitting but will turn his body completely around in a circle to face you while you are circling him. The reason for this behavior is quite simple. The dog wonders what you are doing, where you are going, and what you are going to do when you get there. So he decides to watch and find out. A very successful remedy for this problem is to walk directly in front of the dog and reach down to rub or scratch the sides of his neck with both hands for a few seconds and orally praise him. Then, holding the leash slack, turn aside to your right and proceed around the dog to heeling position. When you are back at heeling position, pet and praise the dog some more.

Problems with the Down Exercise

Two problems occur frequently when you teach this command. First, the dog tries to crawl closer to you. Second, the dog stalls on doing the Down command. Most dogs dislike the Down command, particularly if they are away from you. A dog instinctively feels that he is in a disadvantageous position when he is lying down, as far as escaping or protecting himself from the unexpected is concerned. Consequently, he will try to crawl closer to you, where he may feel more secure, or he will not obey the Down command.

Dog Crawls Closer to Trainer When on the Down Command

Take it as easy as possible with the dog until he has been working a particular command for a couple of days. During that time if the dog tries to crawl closer when on the Down command, go to him and grasp the leash near his neck and slip it under and over the top of one front leg. When he attempts to crawl forward, his weight on the leash puts pressure on his choke collar, which discourages him from trying to crawl.

If the dog continues to crawl toward you after a couple days of practice, give him a fast and firm correction with your foot on the leash (see Fig. 7) and say "Rex, DOWN!" at the same time. While it is not possible to give as firm a correction to a dog that is already lying down as to a dog that sits up or stands, it is still possible to apply enough pressure on his choke collar to show him that he'd better obey your command.

Another way to cure a dog of crawling toward you or stalling on the Down command is to put the six-foot leash on him and stand directly in front of him, working him on the Down and Sit commands for a few minutes. Give him the oral command to sit and if he doesn't do it as soon as you give the command, quickly jerk up on the leash to put him in sitting position. Then say "Rex, DOWN!" and if he doesn't immediately lie down, correct him by using your foot to stamp the leash down, putting him down. Have him do each command in rapid succession, about four times each. Don't give him any time to think about each command. Correct him an instant after you say the command. He should look like a jumping jack—going up, down, up, down. After you have had him do the Sit and Down commands three or four times each, on the last one he does immediately, walk around him to heel position and pet and praise him. Do not use this particular procedure until the dog has had quite a bit of practice on these commands, preferably after off-leash work begins. This procedure will also teach a dog to obey commands promptly.

If none of these methods solves the problem, try giving an on-the-spot correction without going near the dog. Stand as far away from the front of the dog as the six-foot leash will allow but do not put any tension on the leash. Hold the leash in your left hand and when the dog starts crawling toward you on the Down exercise, swing the leash clockwise, exactly as if you were turning a rope for someone to jump. You can hit the dog on the top of his nose with the snap on the end of the leash either lightly or firmly, depending on how hard and how fast you swing the leash. However, the smaller the snap on the leash, the lighter its weight and the less of a correction that can be applied.

Dog Stalls on Doing the Down Command

It is impossible for a dog to stall when you are working him on leash, because you can correct him quickly by putting your foot on the leash (or using the leash correction just described). However, stalling is a common problem when working the dog on distance work with the leash laying on the ground or when off-leash work begins.

By the time you reach that stage of the training, a dog should know the Down command very well. Very often, when a dog is learning to lie down on command, away from you, he will refuse to go down until he sees you are coming to correct him. When he does this, you can be sure he knows what the command means.

Until a dog has had several days of practice of off-leash work, do not correct him for stalling. If the dog doesn't lie down by the time you get to him, correct him. But if he lies down while you are approaching him to correct him, say "Good boy" and continue walking *right past him*. Make a big circle around him and go back to where you were when you gave him the Down command. Praise the dog orally but do not pet him. Never back away from a dog after not correcting him; walk on past him instead.

If the dog is still stalling on the Down command after a couple days, work him for awhile on only the Sit and Down commands. When doing this, continually walk around him in a circle or oval pattern, giving a Sit command, and when he does it follow with the Down command. Have him do each command several times. As you walk around him, giving him these commands, stay no further than about 6 feet from him as you pass him. If he doesn't obey the Sit command, quickly walk up to his side and give him a good, fast Sit correction and quickly walk away to continue your walk around him, giving the Down command next. If the dog stalls on doing the Down command, quickly step up to his side nearest you and give him a fast slap on top of the shoulder with the side of your foot (knocking him down) as you say "Rex, DOWN!" and quickly walk away again. By correcting *fast* and walking away immediately, the dog won't start thinking about running away after being corrected. By continually walking around him as you give him commands and orally praise him for each command he obeys, he also learns to obey immediately because he doesn't know just when you are going to correct him. After you have had him do these commands a few times, return to him by walking around him to heel position and pet and praise him.

Dog Breaks Command after Being Praised

Dogs that tend to break commands will usually do so on the Down command, but they also do it on other commands. Some dogs get the idea that because they were praised for obeying a command, you are not going to enforce your command any further. So they will get up or follow you when you walk away.

Most dogs need a lot of praise and petting to get them to respond. But if your dog gets so excited after being praised that he breaks his command to go to you to get more of it, don't praise him to such an extent that he forgets what he should be doing. Just say "Good boy" and pet him. If your dog gets excited after being petted, give him more oral praise and don't pet him with quite as much enthusiasm. Instead of petting him with your hand as he lies down, rub his side or belly with the bottom of your foot as your stand and praise him verbally. Then walk away; he will usually remain lying down.

Once the dog learns to contain his excitement over the praising and continues to obey the command you have given him, you can then do more praising.

Problems with the Sit Exercise

The most common problem on the sit command is for the dog to move along on his rear to get closer to you and be petted. He will remain sitting and won't lift his rear more than an inch or so from the ground, but he can cover quite a few feet in a matter of seconds. Dogs will often do this when left on a Stay command.

When the dog starts moving, walk farther away from him, stop, turn to face him (not saying a word), and wait a few moments to see what he is going to do. If he stays sitting, forget about it and continue with the lesson. Usually, however, the dog will get up and walk toward you. The dog has then broken his Sit command. Go to him immediately, without saying a word, and take hold of his leash or choke collar and lead him back to where he had originally been left sitting, turn him in a circle to get him facing his original direction, and apply a good, stout Sit correction and say "Rex, SIT!" Promptly walk away from him again and continue with the lesson.

If a dog keeps stalling on doing the Sit command until you go to correct him, put the long leash on and stand about 2 feet in front of him. Have him do the Down and Sit commands repeatedly for a few minutes. Anytime he doesn't obey the command immediately, give him a firm correction. After making him do each command three or four times, pet and praise him.

Problems with Come and Finish Exercises (On Leash)

No problems should exist with the on-leash Come exercise. Those are reserved for after the dog starts to work off leash. The problems encountered with the Finish are usually with the sit or doing the Finish the wrong way or before given the command to do so.

Many dogs, as soon as they begin to get the idea on the Finish, are in a hurry to do it. Some don't want to stop and sit in front of you. They want to hurry directly to heel position instead. Others can't make up their mind—they will rush to heel position, hurry to go and stand in front of you again, or try to go around you again. Some dogs think the whole purpose is to get to the heel position, and surely the fastest way is also the shortest. So instead of going *around* you, they will *back in* to heel position and thereby avoid getting pulled around you. Don't correct your dog if he does this, but be prepared for him to do it the next time. Quickly pull him to your right side and make him go *around* you—the *long* way.

Get the dog to sit in front of you *each time* he comes to you. Stand erect on this exercise (Come and Finish) at all times, bending only to pet the dog or get him to sit properly in front of you. When he starts rushing to get around you, without waiting for the Heel command, be prepared for him. "Catch him" as he comes in by putting both hands on the sides of his neck. Hold his choke collar with the thumb and forefinger of each hand as you scratch his neck with the other fingers and command him to sit. If he doesn't sit, lift up with both hands on the choke collar and he should sit. If not, apply a jerk with the leash. Then pet and praise him for sitting.

If the dog sits more than a foot out in front of you, grasp his choke collar with both hands, at the sides of his neck, and pull him closer. If he sits to either side of you, pull him over in front of you. Orally praise him as you do this to prevent him from thinking that you might be punishing him for coming.

If a dog tries to walk around you without waiting for the Heel command, quickly pull him back in front of you and get him to sit. If he continues trying this, quickly stick your right foot out, catching him on the chest as he tries to go to your right side, then jerk him back in front of you and make him sit. Keep the dog sitting in front of you while you pet him and talk to him for about a minute before you command him to heel. Don't pet him the entire time he is sitting. Talk to him while he sits, then bend down and scratch the sides of his neck. Then stand erect, not touching him, and just orally praise him. If you pet him the entire time before giving him the Heel command, he will immediately begin trying to go to heel position the second you stop. But if you continually praise him orally and pet him two or three separate times before giving him the command to heel, he will learn to remain sitting until you tell him to heel. If you have trouble getting your dog to move behind you, shove his rear behind you with the heel of your right foot and then jerk him to your left side. Command him to sit (and make him do so) when you get him at heeling position.

Sometimes your dog will do the Finish only part way and sit behind you instead of going on to sit at your left side. When your dog does this, turn slightly to your left and finish pulling him around to your left side and make him sit *there*.

Each time you get the dog around you to heel position, make him sit. Give him the Sit command and correct him if he doesn't do it promptly. If he tries to walk past heel position to go in front of you, be prepared for him to try it again and again. Give him a good Sit correction as soon as he starts walking *past* heel position, giving him the oral Sit command at the same time. If you are too slow (or the dog is too fast—which is it?) and he manages to move out in front of you before you correct him, pull him back to proper heel position and correct him to make him sit *there*.

Most people do not know that dogs are "left-handed" or "right-handed" just as people are. The Finish exercise is more difficult for the right-handed dog because it is more natural for them to want to go to their right of you, rather than around you, which is to their left. You can easily tell if your dog is right-handed or left-handed just by playing ball with him. Throw the ball directly away from you into an area in which there are no obstructions in the dog's path. Watch the dog when he picks up the ball and turns to come back to you. A right-handed dog will always turn to his right and a left-handed dog to his left. The only time a dog may not follow this pattern is if there is an object in his way.

Problems with Come and Finish Exercises (Off Leash)
Dog Refuses to Come

When teaching a dog to come off leash, if you give the command to Come and the dog remains where he is, walk up in front of him and apply a sharp jerk forward on his choke collar or shortie leash and say "Rex, COME!" Release your hold immediately after jerking and quickly back away several feet from the dog (still facing the dog). Repeat the hand and oral commands, if necessary. As soon as the dog shows any indication of starting to come, begin praising him in a very happy voice. Pet him really well when you get him in front of you to sit. If the dog still refuses to come to you, your correction must get firmer and your praise must also get better when he does start to come. Correct him every time he does not come on command.

Dog Refuses to Heel

When heeling a dog off leash, if the dog stops walking, quickly stop and turn the upper part of your body toward the dog. Say "Rex, HEEL!" and use the hand command (snapping fingers of left hand or motion forward with a wave of your left hand as you hold it straight down at your side—the reverse of the hand command for the Finish). If necessary, repeat the command a couple of times. If the dog then responds and comes forward toward your left side, immediately begin talking to him in a praising voice. Go only a few steps more, stop, and pet and praise him with plenty of enthusiasm when you get him sitting next to you.

If the dog still does not respond, retrace your steps to his side (heeling position) and correct him by applying a sharp jerk forward on his choke collar (or the shortie leash) and firmly repeat the command as you walk forward. If the dog then starts heeling, immediately begin talking to him in a praising voice and be enthusiastic about your praise and petting when he does the automatic sit at your side.

Follow these procedures any time the dog does not respond to the command to heel. If you have to correct the dog repeatedly for refusing to heel, put the six-foot leash on him for a few minutes and heel him with that, correcting him soundly for any lagging. Then take the long leash off and try him again. You may have to do this repeatedly for a few days until the dog learns to respond. When you have to use the long leash, insist on perfection and correct firmly.

If a dog stops while heeling off leash, it is often your fault. Make sure that you do not wave your arms back and forth as you walk because this will make the dog think that he is being given a Stay command.

Problems with the Finish

Most of the problems with this exercise can be corrected in the same manner as they are in on-leash work. The shortie leash can be used to catch or correct the dog for trying to rush around to heel position without first sitting in front of you or before being commanded to heel for the Finish. You can also check him from trying to go to your right side before being commanded to do so by sticking your right foot out, catching him on the chest, and then jerking him back in front of you and making him sit. If he sits behind you on the Finish, as with on-leash work, move him around with the heel of your right foot or partially turn to your left and jerk him into proper sitting position at your left side with the shortie leash.

There are three methods of correcting the dog that doesn't want to sit at heel position after going around you on the Finish. The first is to quickly grab his choke collar or shortie leash as he starts to walk past his proper sitting position on your left and give him a good backward jerk at a 45-degree angle (Sit correction), jerking back hard enough to put him sitting where he should be. The second method is to quickly stick your left foot out in front of him, catching him on the chest, and make him sit in proper position. The third solution is to give him a Stay command with your left hand just as his head comes forward from behind your left leg. Discontinue this hand command after a day or two or as soon as the dog learns to sit when he gets to heel position.

Problems When Dog is Off Leash
Dog Runs Off

This is a common problem when training a dog to work off leash. It is also a common problem among untrained family dogs. Everything a dog does quickly turns into a habit, so if this is a long-standing problem it is going to be more difficult to correct than if the dog never had the opportunity to acquire the habit.

Many different methods can be used to break a dog of running away and disobeying the Come command. But they all boil down to punishing the dog for not coming. Some obedience trainers go from the six-foot leash to working the dog on commands on a long rope, 15 or 30 feet in length. Some use both, the 15-foot rope and later the 30-foot rope. Then they start working off leash.

I found that it works better and is easier and faster to go directly to off-leash work, but work the dog inside a fence until he is stable. If the necessity for obeying your commands is instilled in his mind inside a fenced yard, he will obey them when he is outside the fence. *A dog does not differentiate between being loose inside a fence and being loose outside a fence. But he does know the difference between being loose and being anchored to you.*

The dog must be corrected every time he runs off. You must catch him and attach the six-foot leash and correct him firmly, according to what he did wrong. If a dog persists in running off, you must be more unrelenting and persistent in your corrections. The correction depends on what he does. If he runs away, breaking a command he is on (such as Sit, Stay, Down, or Stand), he is corrected differently than if he runs when commanded to come or heel.

Dog Runs Off When Commanded to Come

Some dogs will run off when given the command to come. Some will come partway to you and then decide to run. Others will run the instant they hear the word "come." Most dogs will run a few times, at least during their training for off-leash work. If you have a fenced area in which to work your dog, running off doesn't create too much of a problem as it can soon be cured. However, if you have to work your dog in an unfenced area, it is going to be more difficult to catch him when he runs.

Every time the dog runs off when commanded to come, you must go and catch him. Attach the six-foot leash and run or walk very fast with him back to where you had been standing when you gave him the command to come. As you are heading back with the dog, apply three separate, firm jerks forward with the leash. With each jerk, say "Rex, COME!" in a loud and firm voice. When you get back to *where you stood when you gave the command to come*, make the dog sit in front of you, facing you, exactly as he would have been if he had obeyed your command. You and the dog should both be facing in your original directions. Then pet and praise him and give him the Heel command to do the Finish. When he goes around you and sits at heel position, pet and praise him again.

If you have no choice but to train your dog in an unfenced area, you can make a pad to attach to the leash that will assist you in catching him if he runs off frequently. You can make the pad out of a piece of leather that is 6 inches wide and 8 inches long. If you don't have any leather, you could also make it out of about four thicknesses of denim cloth with a piece of thin cardboard in the middle. Round off the corners and make slits in both ends so the pad fits the leash tightly. Slide the pad onto the six-foot leash at a point where it would be directly beneath your dog's loin or hip when he is dragging the leash. When the dog runs off, he will step on this pad with his hind foot, which will cause pressure on his choke collar and make him stop, giving you the opportunity to catch him. If you have to train in an open area and the dog persistently tries to run off, you may have to work him with the leash dragging for a couple of days until you can break him of running. If the dog comes to you occasionally, toss the leash out of his path and call him from short distances because he is likely to step on the pad when he does come.

Dog Runs Off While Heeling

Occasionally your dog will run off when you are heeling him. You must catch the dog, attach the six-foot leash to the choke collar, and take him back to where you were heeling him. Lead the dog back at a fast walk or run, correcting him with three separate jerks forward with the leash. With each jerk, say "Rex, HEEL!" When you get back to where you were when the dog ran off, continue heeling him from that point. But keep him on leash for a few minutes, correcting him when he needs it. Talk to him in a praising voice when he is heeling correctly and pet him enthusiastically after each automatic sit. Then try heeling him off leash again. If he again decides to run off, you must go get him again and correct him firmly with the three jerks forward with the leash as you loudly repeat the oral command.

Any time a dog begins making mistakes on off-leash work, work him on the leash for a little while and soundly correct him when he doesn't obey. Then take him off the leash and try him again. Correction off leash should not be as hard. But if repeated correction off leash is not getting good response from the dog, put the long leash back on for awhile and correct him firmly when he disobeys. Be sure to pet and praise him when he does it right, especially if you have to do a lot of correcting.

Dog Runs Off After Being Corrected

If a dog has to be corrected to make him do a command when he is working off leash, he may run off after receiving the correction. Nervous dogs are most inclined to do this. They must be caught and corrected for the command they broke. They must be corrected in the same manner as the *never* be done until a dog has had plenty of practice so there is no doubt that he knows what he must do. Even though a dog may have been working on a particular command or exercise, if a new variation of that command or exercise is being taught, it takes time for the dog to learn it. A new variation of an exercise is no different than a totally new exercise to a dog. The only difference is that he is able to learn it a little more quickly. But when a dog has been repeatedly worked on the *same exercise* for several days, he should know it. If he begins refusing to do it, he must be corrected.

Usually, dogs that reach this stage will begin disobeying three or four exercises all at the same time. You may get the dog to do the exercise once and then have trouble the next three or four times. When this happens, corrections must be really firm. If you stick with it, severely correcting him when he needs it and petting and praising him thoroughly when he obeys, you will overcome the obstacle. If you don't, your dog will never be well trained.

Anticipating Commands

"Anticipating" means that a dog performs a command or exercise on his own, without waiting to be given the command to do so, or contrary to another command that may be given him. Anticipating can occur in any type of training and on a variety of exercises. It most often occurs on an exercise a dog either likes to do or is anxious to complete for his own reasons, even to secure the praise and petting he expects will follow.

Anticipating is usually caused by training a dog in such a manner that he learns to do certain commands in a particular pattern. When a dog has been taught to do certain commands in a certain routine, it becomes a habit and he does not want to change. Once a dog learns to do something in a particular way, you won't have much control over the situation. In time, you can lose all control over the dog. For a dog to be well trained, he must learn to obey every command—as soon as you give it and only when you give it.

It is much easier to train a dog so that he is unable to expect any routine than it is to break him of anticipating. The only ways he can be broken once he begins anticipating a command are by preventing him from doing the command or by correcting him. Correction can be a sensitive situation because if the dog is punished for doing an exercise he has been taught to do (even though he did it before you gave the command), he will frequently begin refusing to do that exercise when you do command him to do it. Consequently, correction requires some ingenuity on your part and must be done in such a way that the dog cannot connect the punishment to the exercise he was anticipating. I call such corrections "accidents." There are dog that runs off when on a command of Sit, Stay, Down, or Stand. How ever, after correcting these dogs, really pet and praise them when you g them back into position at the spot from which they ran. These dogs need lot of praise and petting to give them self-confidence.

Dog Runs Off When on a Stay, Sit, Down, or Stand Command

Any time a dog runs off when working on one of these commands, you must go catch him and attach the long leash to his choke collar. Lead him back to where he was when he broke his command and turn him so he is facing the original direction. Then give him a firm correction for the com-mand he broke. If it was a Down command, firmly force him down with your foot on the leash as you say "Rex, DOWN!" Drop the leash and walk away from him for a few moments. Then return to him to pet him and remove the leash. Whatever command he broke when he ran off must be the command for which he is corrected; place him in the position of that command. If the dog runs off three or four times in a row, correct him more firmly each time. Work him on the leash for awhile and correct him soundly whenever he does not immediately obey a command when you are working him on the leash. Remember, as the correction must get harder to secure obedience, so must the praising and petting get better.

Rebellion Problems

At a certain stage of training, a phase is encountered that could be called a "power struggle." In this training method, it is usually encountered around the seventh day of training, but this can vary slightly, depending on the dog and his progression. In slower training procedures, it would likely occur after a number of weeks of training, since it usually occurs when a dog has assimilated a certain amount of training.

It is an attitude of rebellion on the part of the dog. With some dogs, the phase comes and goes almost unnoticed. With other dogs, it can become a real contest to determine who is going to get the upper hand—the dog or the trainer.

Most people don't understand what has happened to their dog. He sud-denly stops being even reasonably dependable on commands on which he has been working, and repeated correction often has no effect. It is a frustrat-ing period for most trainers, and they feel the dog just isn't capable of learning.

When the dog reaches the point when he will not obey commands he has been repeatedly practiced on for a few days, you must correct him emphati-cally every time he breaks a command or refuses to do one. But this should many different possible "accidents," but they have to be geared to the dog and the exercise he is anticipating. You must pet and console the dog after he has met with an "accident."

In obedience work, a dog can develop the habit of anticipating commands, coming closer, or coming directly to you when you are working him simply because of the way he is handled at other times when he is not on command. For example, if a person in contact with the dog frequently speaks the dog's name and then pets or praises the dog when he comes, merely on hearing his name, the dog may soon begin coming toward you as soon as you say his name when you are working him on his exercises. He will not wait to see if a command is going to be given after his name is spoken. This also encourages a dog to begin performing actions or exercises on his own, according to what and when he thinks it should be done.

If a dog has been correctly trained and he begins doing something when he is not on command and you shout his name, the dog should stop and turn his head to look at you, waiting for your command. Then you give him a command. This is correct and the dog should not be punished for pausing to await your command.

Dog Anticipates on Come, Sit, or Down Exercises

If a dog has been worked on commands in a set pattern, which people tend to do for dog show competition in particular, the dog is very likely to begin anticipating, especially on the Finish, Sit, Down, or Come exercises. The dog knows the next command you have usually been giving him and will often do it as soon as you say his name, before you say the command word. The dog can be broken of this habit; however, if you continue to work your dog in a set pattern, he will soon begin anticipating again.

If the dog frequently comes toward you when you are working him on commands although you have not given the Come command, have the six-foot leash handy. The instant the dog begins coming toward you, quickly go to him and attach the leash to his choke collar. Apply a firm jerk in the direction from which the dog came and then lead him back to the spot he had been. Turn him so he is facing his original direction and give him a good correction for the command he was on, putting him in that position. Then stand next to him at heeling position. (If the dog was anticipating on the Sit or Down commands, also attach the leash and stand at heeling position.)

Work the dog on Sit and Down commands as you stand next to him, at heeling position, with the dog on leash. Have the dog do each command four or five times, in the following manner.

Begin with the dog in sitting position. As he remains sitting, say "Rex, (pause to the mental count of ten) DOWN!" As you say the word "down" apply a light to moderate correction with your foot on the leash, putting the dog down. Leave him down for three or four seconds, without saying anything. Then say, "Rex, (pause again to the mental count of ten) SIT!" As you say the word "sit," apply a light to moderate upward jerk on the leash. Do this four or five times with each command. When you finish, pet and praise him. If the dog attempts to sit or lie down while you are pausing, he must be immediately corrected and put back in the position of his last command. This procedure teaches the dog that he must wait until you actually give him the command and then he must do it immediately.

When you have finished having him do the Sits and Downs at heel position, give him a Stay command and walk out in front of him a distance of 4 or 5 feet and again have him do the Sit and Down commands but do not give him a correction unless he doesn't do each command immediately. Use the same procedure of giving his name and then pausing before you say the command word. The dog should also be on leash when doing this so he can be quickly corrected, if necessary. If the dog should attempt to come to you when working him on these Sits and Downs, immediately correct him firmly, putting him back in position of the command he broke. Do likewise if he changes his position. For example, if he was on a Sit command and laid down while you were pausing, quickly jerk him back up to sitting position. After you have made him do each command four or five times, go around him to heeling position to pet and praise him well, but make sure you return to him after a command he did correctly.

After working the dog on these two procedures, you can again try working him off leash at a distance of about 15 feet. Again, give his name loudly and then pause before you say the command word. If the dog does the commands well, go and pet him and take him off command for a few minutes with the Okay command. But if he again begins making mistakes on any exercise by coming to you or doing a command before you tell him to, repeat these instructions.

Appendix

Photo Review
of
Training Exercises

Heeling With Automatic Sit Exercise

The oral command to sit is given as the trainer applies jerks at a 45-degree angle toward the dog's rear and pushes the dog's rump down, using the instep of the right foot.

The Okay hand command that releases the dog from command.

Lesson 2

Sit/Stay Exercise

Stay hand command when given at the heeling position beside the dog.

Stay hand command when given away from the dog.

When the dog breaks from the sit position and stands up or attempts to go to the trainer, he must be promptly put back into the sitting position by applying a jerk on the leash angled toward his rear.

To return to the heel position, the trainer walks slightly to his right and circles the dog's rear (stepping over his tail). The leash must not touch or drag on the dog.

The trainer walks forward and stands to the dog's right side (heeling position). The trainer then pets and praises the dog.

Lesson 3

Down Exercise, Away from Dog

The beginning of the Down hand command.

The completion of the Down hand command.

Teaching the Down exercise away from the trainer by using foot pressure on the leash to place the dog in the down position.

Lesson 4

Down and Sit Exercise, Away from Dog and at Heel Position

The beginning of the Sit hand command.

The completion of the Sit hand command.

Teaching the Sit exercise away from the trainer by swinging the leash upward as the hand and oral commands are given.

Teaching the Down exercise at the heel position with foot pressure on the leash (using the oral command).

Lesson 5
Come (Recall) and Finish Exercise

To begin the on-leash Come exercise, the trainer faces the dog from a distance of about 5 feet while the dog remains on a Sit/Stay command. Dog is orally praised for a few moments.

The trainer gives the Come command (hand and oral) and applies little, short jerks on the leash until the dog begins coming toward him. The command and oral praise are rotated while getting the dog to come.

The dog is placed in the sitting position after coming to the trainer by applying a mild jerk on the leash at a 45-degree angle toward the rear of the dog.

The trainer orally praises the dog as the dog is kept sitting for a few moments.

The trainer pets and praises the dog for coming while he loosens the choke collar.

The beginning hand command for the Finish at Heel exercise.

The completion of the Finish at Heel hand command.

After giving the hand and oral commands to heel, the dog's leash is switched to the trainer's right hand. The trainer then takes one step back with his right foot.

The dog is then pulled to the trainer's right rear.

The trainer switches the leash, behind him, to his left hand and takes one step forward with his right foot, while pulling the dog forward to the trainer's left side.

With his right foot, the trainer moves the dog's rear so the dog is in a straight line at the trainer's left side.

While giving the oral Sit command, the trainer jerks the leash at a 45-degree angle toward the dog's rear as he pushes the dog's rump down with the instep of his right foot.

The dog is now in the proper sitting position at heel.

The trainer praises and pets the dog as he loosens the choke collar.

Lesson 6

Stay While Heeling Exercise (Motion Exercise)

To teach the Stay While Heeling exercise, the trainer tosses the leash aside as the oral and hand commands to stay are given.

After tossing the leash aside, the trainer continues to walk away while the dog stays.

Lesson 7

Beginning Distance Training

To begin distance training, the trainer walks about 10 feet away from the dog and works him on all the commands he has previously learned. If the dog responds correctly, the distance should be increased by 5 feet and the commands repeated. The trainer should pet and praise the dog after every correct response. The photos illustrate working the dog on the Sit and Down commands.

Lesson 8

Beginning Off-Leash Work

The trainer begins off-leash training by walking about 10 feet away from the dog.

The dog is commanded to come with both oral and hand commands.

Dog completes the exercise by sitting in front of the trainer. The trainer should always pet and praise the dog after every correct exercise.

To begin the Finish at Heel exercise off-leash, give the dog the Heel command. Some dogs will attempt the Finish exercise before they have been given the command. The trainer must catch and correct the dog with the shortie leash or choke collar before the dog returns to the heel position.

Lesson 9

Stand Exercise

The beginning of the hand command for the Stand exercise.

The end of the sideways hand motion for the Stand exercise.

The trainer teaches the Stand exercise by using his foot to lift the dog into a standing position while applying little jerks on the leash in a forward and upward direction.

Lesson 10

Teaching the Dog to Come When Not On Command and Starting Distraction Work

To begin on-leash distraction training, the trainer puts a six-foot leash on the dog so he cannot run off to chase the distraction. Each dog has its own form of distraction so you must experiment to determine what interests your dog. A cat is used in these examples. The dog should be worked on all the commands he has learned. When a command is given, the dog must obey immediately or take a firm correction. The trainer should pet and praise the dog when he responds properly.

Down (Drop) on Recall (Motion Exercise)

To teach the Down (Drop) on Recall exercise, the trainer stands about 10 feet away from the dog. The trainer faces the dog and stamps his foot to encourage the dog to respond to the command. The dog should stay in the down position until another command is given.

Lesson 12

Sit on Recall (Motion Exercise)

While the dog is on the stay command, the trainer walks 25 to 30 feet in front of him, then turns and faces him. The trainer praises the dog orally and then gives the Come command. When the dog is one third to one half the distance to you, give the hand and oral Sit commands. After the dog has remained in the sit position for a few moments, the trainer again commands him to come.

Lesson 13

Stay on Recall (Motion Exercise)

While the dog is walking toward the trainer on the Come command, the trainer gives him the Stay command. After stopping and staying for a few moments, the dog should be given another command and then finish at heel. If the dog performs properly, the trainer should pet and praise him.

Lesson 14

Off-Leash Distraction Work

If the dog is well trained in on-leash distraction work from lesson 10, he should have no difficulty with off-leash distraction training. However, off-leash distraction work may require a little more time and effort. While the dog is off-leash, the trainer gives him several hand and oral commands while a distraction is nearby. If he obeys the commands, the trainer should give him plenty of praise and affection.

Index

A

Anticipating command, 120-122
Attention, lack of, 15-16
Automatic sit command, 106-108

B

Biting in training, 18-21
Biting leash in training, 104

C

Cats in distraction work
  off leash, 99-101
  on leash, 84-86
Choke collar, 7-8
Come command, 53-60
  anticipation of, 121-122
  correction for, 29
  definition of, 23
  hand command for, 28, 55
  when not on command, 80-87
  off leash, 73-74
  problems with, 113-116
  refusal to obey, 115
  running off during, 117-118
Come and finish exercise, 53-60, 73-74, 113-116
Command
  anticipating, 120-122
  breaking after praise, 112-113
  refusal to do, 17
  wrong, 17
Concentration of dog, 4
Control of dog, 24-25
Correction
  for come command, 29

Correction—cont'd
  for down command, 29
  for finish command, 29
  foot, 83-84
  for forward command, 29
  for heel command, 29
  proper use of, 27-31
  running off after, 118-119
  for sit command, 29
  for stand command, 29
  for stay command, 29
Cowering in training, 17-18
Crawling in training, 17-18, 110-111
Crowding trainer, 105
Crying in training, 17

D

Distance training, 65-68
Distraction work, 80-87
  cats in
    off leash, 99-101
    on leash, 84-86
  definition of, 24
  food in
    off leash, 101-102
    on leash, 86-87
  meat in
    off leash, 101-102
    on leash, 86-87
  off leash, 99-102
Dogs
  psychology of, 2-6
  sign language of, 2-3
Down command, 43-47, 48-52
  anticipation of, 121-122

Down command—cont'd
  away from dog, 43-47
  correction for, 29
  definition of, 23
  hand command for, 28, 45
  off leash, 72-73, 88-91
  problems with, 110-113
  running off during, 119
Down (drop) on recall exercise, 88-91
Down and sit exercise, 48-52

E

Equipment, training, 6-8
Exercise
  come and finish, 53-60, 73-74, 113-116
  down
    away from dog, 43-47
    problems with, 110-113
    on recall, 88-91
    and sit, 48-52
  heeling
    with automatic sit, 32-36
    off leash, 71-72
  motion, 27, 61-64
    definition of, 23
    down on recall, 88-91
    sit on recall, 92-94
    stay on recall, 95-98
  scent discrimination, 27
  sit
    problems with, 113-115
    on recall, 92-94
    stay, and down, 72-73
  sit/stay, 37-42
  stand, 75-79
  stay
    on recall, 95-98
    while heeling, 61-64, 73

F

Fidgeting in training, 17
Fighting leash in training, 103-104
Finish and come exercise, 53-60, 73-74, 113-116
Finish command, 53-60
  correction for, 29
  definition of, 23
  hand command for, 28
  off leash, 73-74
  problems with, 113-116
Food in distraction work
  off leash, 101-102
  on leash, 86-87

Foot correction, 83-84
Forward command
  correction for, 29
  hand command for, 28

G

Growling in training, 18-21

H

Hand commands in training, 25-26
  for come command, 28, 55
  for down command, 28, 45
  for finish command, 28
  for forward command, 28
  for heel command, 28
  for okay command, 28, 36
  for sit command, 28, 49, 50
  for stand command, 28, 77
  for stay command, 28, 39, 40, 62
Hard-headed dog, 8-9, 21-22
Heel command, 32-36, 41-42, 61-64, 110
  with automatic sit, 32-36
  correction for, 29
  definition of, 23
  hand command for, 28
  off leash, 71-72, 73
  problems in, 103-106
  refusal to obey, 115-116
  running off during, 118
Hiding in training, 15
Hierarchy of dogs, 3-4

I

Incorrect pivot by trainer, 103
Intelligence of dogs, 6

J

Jumping on trainer, 105-106

L

Laying ears back in training, 16
Leash biting in training, 104
Leash fighting in training, 103-104
Leather leash, 6-7
Locking eyes, 3
Looking away in training, 16
Lying down in training, 16, 108

M

Meat in distraction work
  off leash, 101-102
  on leash, 86-87
Mental block in training, 5

Motion exercises, 27, 61-64
  definition of, 23
  down on recall, 88-91
  sit on recall, 92-94
  stay on recall, 95-98

O

Off command, 36
Off-leash come command, 73-74
Off-leash distraction work, 23, 69-74, 99-102,
  116-119
Off-leash down command, 72-73, 88-91
Off-leash finish command, 73-74
Off-leash heel command, 71-72, 73
Off-leash recall command, 88-91, 92-94, 95-98
Off-leash sit command, 72-73, 92-94
Off-leash stand command, 75-79
Off-leash stay command, 72-73, 95-98
Okay command, 36
  hand command for, 28, 36

P

Perfect sits, 24
Pivot, incorrect, by trainer, 103
Praise, breaking command after, 112-113
Problems in training, 103-122
Psychology, dog, 2-6
Pulling ahead in training, 104

R

Reactions of dogs to training, 15-22
Rebellion problems, 119-120
Recall command, 53-60
  definition of, 23
  down on, 88-91
  off leash, 88-91, 92-94, 95-98
Recall and finish exercise, 53-60
Return exercise, 108-110
Running in training, 15
Running off, 116-117
  during come command, 117-118
  after correction, 118-119
  during down command, 119
  during heel command, 118
  during sit command, 119
  during stand command, 119
  during stay command, 119

S

Scent discrimination exercise, 27
Sign language of dogs, 2-3
Sit
  perfect, 24

Sit—cont'd
  on recall exercise, 92-94
Sit command, 32-36, 37-42, 48-52
  anticipation of, 121-122
  correction for, 29
  definition of, 23
  hand command for, 28, 49, 50
  off leash, 72-73, 92-94
  problems with, 106-108, 113-115
  refusal to obey, 106
  running off during, 119
Sit/stay exercise, 37-42
Sitting
  ahead of trainer, 107
  at angle in front of trainer's legs, 107
  crooked, 107-108
  to rear of trainer, 106-107
  too far away from trainer, 107
Skin twist, 84
Snapping in training, 18-21
Stalling in training, 111-112
Stand command
  correction for, 29
  definition of, 23
  hand command for, 28, 77
  off leash, 75-79
  running off during, 119
Standing on trainer's foot, 108
Staring, 3
State of mind, dog's, 4
Stay(ing)
  behind trainer, 104
  while heeling exercise, 61-64, 73
  on recall exercise, 95-98
Stay command, 37-42, 61-64
  correction for, 29
  definition of, 23
  hand command for, 28, 39, 40, 62
  off leash, 72-73, 95-98
  running off during, 119
Stubbornness, 8-9, 21-22
Submission, 3

T

Trainer
  attempting to get between legs of, 104-105
  attempting to go to or touch, 109-110
  attempting to walk on right side of, 105
  crowding, 105
  incorrect pivot by, 103
  jumping on, 105-106
  pulling ahead of, 104
  sitting ahead of, 107

Trainer—cont'd
   sitting at angle in front of legs of, 107
   sitting to rear of, 106-107
   standing in front of, 108
   staying behind, 104
Training
   basics of, 1-10
   common mistakes in, 8-10
   distance, 65-68
   equipment for, 6-8
   problems in, 103-122
   reactions of dogs to, 15-22

Training—cont'd
   successful, rules for, 31
   tips for, 11-14
Turning around as trainer returns to heel
   position, 110
Turning head from side to side, 17

W
Whining in training, 17-18

Y
Yelping in training, 17